THE HIGHLANDS AND ISLANDS OF
SCOTLAND

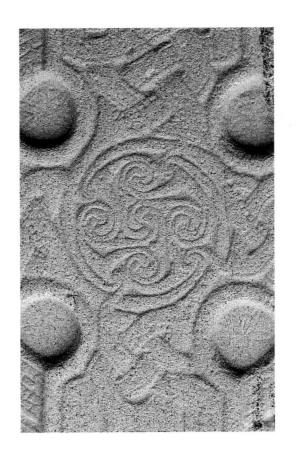

THE HIGHLANDS AND ISLANDS OF
SCOTLAND

Text by Angus Macdonald
Photographs by Patricia Macdonald

Foreword by *George Mackay Brown*

CASSELLPAPERBACKS

First published in the United Kingdom in 1991 by
Weidenfeld & Nicolson Ltd

This paperback edition first published in 2001 by
Cassell Paperbacks, Cassell & Co
Wellington House, 125 Strand
London, WC2R 0BB

Distributed in the United States of America by
Sterling Publishing Co., Inc.
387 Park Avenue South,
New York, NY 10016-8810

A CIP catalogue record for this book is available
from the British Library

ISBN 1-84188-154-6

Designed by Nick Avery
Printed and bound in Italy

Half-title page: Early Christian carved stone, Ardchattan Priory (see p. 60)
Title page: Above Braeriach, Cairngorms

CONTENTS

ACKNOWLEDGMENTS

Patricia and Angus Macdonald would like to thank all those, too numerous to mention, who have assisted in the making of this book. Special thanks are due to the following people whose knowledge, kindness and courtesy have made our recent travels in the Highlands and Islands particularly interesting and enjoyable: James Logan and Mr D. C. Mair of Glenfiddich Distillery; Hector McAulay; Donald Macdonald; Ian MacGregor (senior and junior); Mr R. MacKinnon; Mr and Mrs Iain McVean; Eric Ross; John Macleod, Joan McDonald, Dollag MacLean, Pat MacFarlane, Duncan Morrison, Margaret Hulse; Annie and John McQueen, Iain and Dolly MacMillan and family, Katie MacLean, Harriet MacIsaac; Maria and David Chamberlain; Mahala Andrews, Hugh Cheape, David Caldwell; members of the Scottish Wild Land Group, especially Anne Macintyre; Dave Morris of the Ramblers' Association; Adam Watson; staff of the Nature Conservancy Council, especially Rawdon Goodier (Edinburgh), Dave Gowans and Chris Strachan (Creag Meagaidh Reserve), and Tim Clifford (Ben Eighe Reserve); members of the John Muir Trust, especially Terry Isles, Paul and Margaret Jarvis, and Denis Mollison; Simon Pepper of the World Wild Fund for Nature; staff of Air Traffic Control and Met. Offices at Inverness, Stornoway and Benbecula; Dave and Pauline Howitt, Mrs Scott-Howitt; J. Gordon and Muriel Macintyre; Helen and Willie Morrison; Rod and Gerry Stenson; Iain Morrison of *Turus Mara* and Murdo Grant of M V *Shearwater*.

We should also like to thank the staff of Weidenfeld & Nicolson, particularly Colin Grant, editor, and Nick Avery, designer, for their hard work and patience.

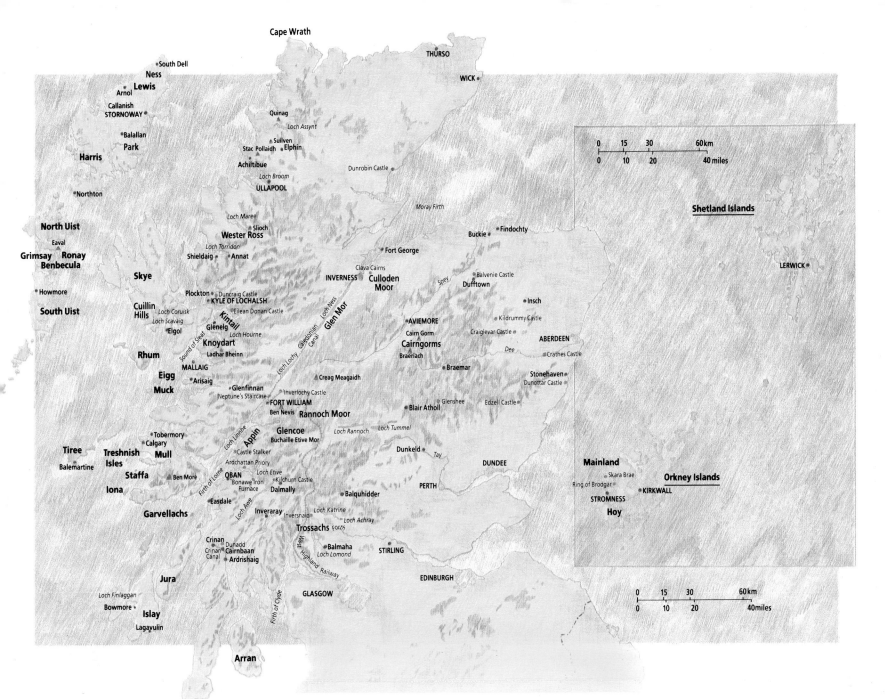

Cape Wrath

THURSO

WICK

South Dell
Ness
Lewis
Arnol
Callanish
STORNOWAY

Quinag
Loch Assynt

Balallan
Park

Suilven
Stac Pollaidh   Elphin
Achiltibue
Loch Broom
ULLAPOOL

Dunrobin Castle

Harris

Northton

Moray Firth

North Uist

Loch Maree
Slioch
Wester Ross
Loch Torridon
Shieldaig   Annat

Buckie   Findochty

Fort George

Grimsay   Ronay
Benbecula

Skye

Clava Cairns
INVERNESS   Culloden
Moor

Balvenie Castle
Spey   Dufftown

LERWICK

Shetland Islands

Howmore

Plockton   Duncraig Castle
KYLE OF LOCHALSH
Eilean Donan Castle

Insch

South Uist

Cuillin
Hills
Loch Coruisk
Loch Scavaig
Elgol

Kintail
Glenelg
Loch Hourne

AVIEMORE
Cairn Gorm
Cairngorms
Braeriach

Kildrummy Castle
Craigievar Castle

ABERDEEN

Rhum

Knoydart
Ladhar Bheinn

Dee

Crathes Castle

Eigg
MALLAIG
Muck
Arisaig

Creag Meagaidh

Braemar

Stonehaven
Dunottar Castle

Glenfinnan
Neptune's Staircase   Inverlochy Castle
FORT WILLIAM
Ben Nevis   Rannoch Moor

Blair Atholl

Glenshee
Edzell Castle

Tiree
Tobermory
Calgary

Treshnish
Isles   Mull
Balemartine

Appin   Glencoe
Castle Stalker   Buchaille Etive Mor
Ardchattan Priory

Loch Rannoch   Loch Tummel

Dunkeld
Tay

DUNDEE

Mainland
Skara Brae
Ring of Brodgar   KIRKWALL

Orkney Islands

Staffa
Ben More
OBAN
Bonawe Iron
Furnace
Easdale

Loch Etive
Kilchurn Castle
Dalmally

Balquhidder

PERTH

STROMNESS
Hoy

Iona

Garvellachs

Inveraray
Inversnaid
Loch Awe

Loch Katrine
Loch Achray

Crinan
Crinan   Dunadd
Canal   Cairnbaan
Ardrishaig

Trossachs   Forth

Balmaha
Loch Lomond

STIRLING

Jura

Loch Finlaggan
Bowmore
Islay
Lagavulin

West Highland Railway

Firth of Clyde

EDINBURGH

GLASGOW

Arran

0   15   30   60km
0   10   20   40 miles

0   15   30   60km
0   10   20   40miles

FOREWORD

Loch Coruisk and the Black Cuillins, Skye

The Black Cuillins are some of Scotland's wildest and most romantic mountains. The spectacular ice-carved trough which contains Loch Coruisk is almost surrounded by their frost-shattered cliffs, pinnacles and scree-slopes.

Strangely, it was out of defeat that the Highlands of Scotland became a symbol of beauty and high romance. On a cold April day in 1746 the remnants of Prince Charles Edward Stuart's army were crushed by the disciplined Hanoverian army at Culloden moor near Inverness. That, it seemed, was 'the end of an old song'. The Highland clans had never had much respect for the authorities in London, or in Edinburgh either. They were a separate proud people with their own loyalties and language and ancient ceremonies.

The clans were seen as a perpetual threat to the establishment, and earlier attempts had been made to overawe them: the Glencoe massacre, for example. But the defeat at Culloden was the final hammer-blow.

The Gaelic peoples have the gift of transmuting suffering and defeat into beauty. The hunting of Prince Charles Edward by the redcoats through the mountains and islands, which he and his handful of men bore with such cheerfulness, and his final escape on a French ship, touched the imagination of the people and begot a hundred beautiful poems and songs, so that even the next generation of Englishmen was moved by the endurance and the heroism.

This rapid myth-making coincided with the surging wave all through Europe of romanticism. The wild lonely places of the world meant freedom and delight for the human spirit that was, by the beginning of the nineteenth century, beginning to chafe at the ugliness of industrialism and the grime and unwholesomeness of the new cities. Wordsworth and Keats were beginning now to write the poetry of nature and wonderment that the Highland poets had been harping from time immemorial. The urban verse of Pope and Samuel Johnson was suddenly unfashionable. Dr Johnson and his contemporaries had seen mountains and lochs as gross ugly excrescences; the skill of landscape gardeners and poets had been to tame nature to the acceptable measurements of man.

Now, romanticism had set the imagination free again, and a great outpouring of literature – Scott, Byron – extolled the wild beauty of the Highlands, and the bravery and loyalty of its people. That delight has never been extinguished.

Painters and composers and writers from all over Europe came for inspiration to the Highlands. *The Monarch of the Glen* and 'Fingal's Cave' are by-products of this romantic urge.

At the same time, the huge economic forces generated in the exchanges and counting houses of London spread wider and wider and induced a weakening of the loyalty between chief and clanspeople. Money was now the measure. It was more economical for the great landowners – many of them educated at English public schools and universities – to have the glens populated by flocks of Cheviot sheep than by the easy-going and imaginative people who had been so loyal to them in the past, through every conceivable misery and misfortune. Then began the evictions, the burning roof-trees, the mass emigration to Canada and Australia and New Zealand. The clans were broken. The speaking of a beautiful language was discouraged. The glens and the shores emptied rapidly.

Still, as this book abundantly shows, the magnificent scenery of the Highlands can never be subtracted from the sum of things. A turn of the political and economic wheel brought about the thinning of the population.

Another turn of the wheel may well bring people back to the lonely straths; but 'the old song', the culture anciently rooted, can never be restored.

*

With the Scottish islands to the west and north, the story is different. The mainland Highlanders are predominantly Celts, like the Irish, the Welsh, the people of Cornwall and Brittany. Orkney and Shetland and Lewis became increasingly populated by Norwegians from the eighth or ninth century onward. To begin with, these Vikings arrived by stealth, as raiders; but seeing how fertile some of the islands – Orkney, certainly – were, they took over the land and settled as farmers and traders, ruled over by earls who owed allegiance to the Norwegian crown. The islanders spoke their own language, Norn, and their literature consisted of magnificent stories about the Earls of Orkney and their friends and enemies: *The Orkneyinga Saga*. There is a wide gulf between the spare dramatic saga narrative and the songs and poetry of the Gaels: an indication of how different those northern Scottish races were. Often the Norse islanders and the Celtic highlanders were at war with each other.

> The stone of the battlement
> Laid in the heather.
>
> Loch water laves
> The high white stone, the lintel.

Little walks in a Celtic keep now
But four grey winds.

Where is the harp,
Heart of the proud dance in winter?

Where are fire, the round silver plate?
Where the ancient courtesy?

The last guests in this place
Were Thorfinn's soldiers.

Can the runes of verse
Celebrate victory, and restore
A broken stone web?

Increasingly, as the centuries passed, Orkney and Shetland and the Hebrides were drawn into the orbit of Scotland. The defeat of King Hakon of Norway at Largs in Ayrshire in 1263 marked the true end of Scandinavian authority in the islands; the king died that same winter in the Bishop's Palace in Kirkwall, Orkney.

Those islanders were more than sea-reivers and pirates. They had a rough-and-ready code of law, hewn out at their regular assemblies (or 'things') of the chief landowners and merchants. They loved the ale-cups and fires and stories and laughter of winter nights. Above all, they worked the land industriously, as can be seen in the green fertile Orkneys. The boldest of them were not above an annual Viking cruise between plough-time and harvest-time, long after the main Viking thrust had petered out.

The unexpected climax to a turbulent history was the emergence of an earl who was seen as a martyr after his killing on Egilsay island in 1117: Saint Magnus. Not long afterwards architect and masons began work on St Magnus Cathedral in Kirkwall, and his nephew Rognvald – in many ways the greatest of Orcadians – set out on an adventure-strewn crusade to Jerusalem, Byzantium, and Rome.

Orkney and Shetland were absorbed into Scotland in 1468, and after that the sagamen ceased to give utterance, though the tongues at the winter fires have never been silent, and Orkney writers have always been prominent in the literature of Scotland; Shetlanders have contributed richly with music, especially fiddle-music.

Two world wars – the British fleet used Scapa Flow in Orkney as its main base – and the discovery of oil in the North Sea near Shetland have of recent years greatly altered the northern islands' economy. There is a continuing flight of people from the cities of the south into the tranquillity of the western and northern islands. But racial admixtures are the norm in all civilizations, and on the whole make for healthy communities; once the initial shock is absorbed, a second generation of 'in-comers' speaks in the same accents as the 'natives', and subscribes to the same values.

This book is a testament to a rich, many-faceted culture and to a beautiful interweave of land and mountain and waters.

George Mackay Brown
December 1990

Farm near Balmaha Loch Lomond

The transition between the Lowlands and the Highlands (the 'Highland Line') may be readily experienced at the Pass of Balmaha on the road which runs along the eastern shore of Loch Lomond beween Drymen and Rowardennan. The small farm shown here, which is situated just to the north-west of the pass, is the first on the Highland side of the Line, and the sharp ridge of the hill to the right (Conic Hill) lies on the Line itself.

The Highland Line marks, in a physical sense, a change in scenery which is a consequence of a change in the nature of the underlying rocks (see also the photograph on p.14). Many would say that it also marks, however, a boundary which relates to other, less tangible but fundamental differences which exist within Scotland, differences in attitudes, priorities, culture and history which make the Highlands in many ways a separate country from the Lowlands.

Land and Wildlife

**The 'Highland Line'
Loch Lomond**

Four of the thirty islands in Loch
Lomond lie on the 'Highland
Line', that distinct division, which
runs from the Mull of Kintyre in
the south-west to Stonehaven on
the east coast, between the gentle
countryside of the Central
Lowlands and the more rugged,
mountainous terrain of the
Highlands. The line, known to
geologists as the 'Highland
Boundary Fault', may be clearly
seen here, expressed as a ridge in
the landscape. The older, harder
rocks of the Highlands are seen on
the left of the picture and the more
recently formed, softer
sedimentary deposits of the
Lowlands on the right.

'If I tried to remember the outstanding beauties and chief points of interest in this won-
derful island, my writing would degenerate into a mere list of names', wrote the poet
Hugh MacDiarmid, speaking of the Isle of Skye, one single island in the Hebrides. The
coastline of Scotland is so ragged that it breaks up on the north and west into more than
eight hundred islands, 'not counting the innumerable skerries which are only little
snaggles of rock jutting out of the water'. And the mainland is as fragmented in other
ways, and as full of interest as the islands. This chapter gives a small sample only, therefore, of the rich variety of landscape experience which may be encountered by the traveller in the Highlands and Islands of Scotland.

Many types of mountain are here: the black craggy peaks of the Cuillins of Skye; the
ice-worn, rounded, dissected plateau of the Cairngorms; formidable ranges such as those
of Glencoe or Kintail; single mountains standing proud of the surrounding landscape, as
in Assynt. The scale of these is not large in relation to that of the Alps or the Rockies but,
in the absence of direct comparison, this is not significant. They certainly offer the gran-
dest scenery in the British Isles, and some of the most beautiful in the world.

For the connoisseur of landscape there is much else besides: the region is also famous
for the incomparable seascapes and spectacular cliffs of the north and west; the long,
lonely beaches of pure white sand of the Outer Hebrides; the flat boglands and wild
moorlands, stretching to every horizon, of the north and centre; and the lush wide straths
and fertile rolling fields of the north-eastern coastal plains.

The reason for this impressive diversity lies in the geology, the way in which the land
was formed. The Scottish Highlands have been carved from some of the most complicated
geological structures on Earth so it is no accident that they are a classic region for the
study of geology and scenery, or that so many fundamental geological discoveries have
been made, historically, by Scottish geologists.

The oldest rocks are those of the Western Isles and the ancient north-western 'foreland', from Torridon to Cape Wrath. The 'Lewisian' gneiss, named after the island of
Lewis, was formed between 2000 and 3000 million years ago and was metamorphosed by
heat and pressure deep in the roots of a long-vanished mountain range. These rocks are
now found on both sides of the Atlantic Ocean, but they date from times when the
patterns of land and sea were quite different from today. The rivers from these ancient

mountains flowed eastward to deposit on the bed of a sea masses of sand, later to become the 'Torridonian' sandstones of the mountains which now stretch along the north-west coast of Scotland. Over many millions of years of erosion the sandstones were gradually worn down and the gneiss was exposed. These two bands of rock, the gneiss and the Torridonian sandstone, formed a solid mass against which younger rocks to the south and east were crumpled up in waves which ran from south-west to north-east in an episode of mountain building activity which took place 400 million years ago.

Only the worn-down stumps of these ancient mountains – once as mighty as the Himalayas are today – now remain, due to the action of wind, water and extremes of temperature through the intervening ages. Ice sheets were the greatest of these modifying forces, and they have left behind the full panoply of glaciated landscape – corries, U-shaped valleys, hanging valleys, moraines. Frost action too has played its part and has left rugged craggy peaks.

This land has also been the scene of much volcanic activity. Some of the prominent mountains, such as Ben More on Mull, are themselves the remains of old volcanoes and others such as Ben Nevis owe their existence to the result of volcanic activity on sedimentary rocks.

The natural history of the Highlands has been determined by the combination of geology, climate and human activity. The natural vegetation over most of the mainland and the Inner Hebrides would be forest: Scots pine, or oak with an undercover of holly and hazel on the sunnier slopes and at lower levels on the best soils. Sadly, most of this woodland has gone, a victim of the axe and of fires of both natural and human origin, the latter being both deliberate and accidental. A few remnants of the pinewood remain, those at Rothiemurchus and the Black Wood of Rannoch being fine examples, and there are relict oakwoods as well, such as those on the eastern shores of Loch Lomond. Most of the landscape now has a denuded appearance, however, and where substantial woodland does exist it is mostly found in the form of commercial monoculture plantations of alien species, such as Sitka spruce.

The western Highlands are the wettest part of Europe. Without the protection of a forest canopy the land quickly becomes saturated and this, together with the acid soils which result from the underlying gneiss, schist or granite, produces conditions which are ideal for the establishment of blanket bog. Heather and sphagnum moss grow well in this situation and rot down to form thick layers of peat in which little else will grow. The resulting, rather forbidding landscape – a kind of wet desert – has a wild and forlorn look which is now part of the character of the Highland region. It is seen to good effect on the great Moor of Rannoch and in the vast flat wetlands of 'Flow Country' of Caithness and Sutherland.

Where lime-rich shell sand has become mixed with the acid soils, as on the western seaboard of the Outer Hebrides and in isolated pockets elsewhere, a particularly rich flora results with sweet green grass and a profusion of wild flowers in the spring and early summer. These are the *machairs*, which are one of the glories of the region.

The bird life of the Highlands and Islands is rich, the most spectacular concentrations being the breeding colonies of seabirds on the coastal cliffs. Inland, the birds of prey are well represented, chief amongst these being the golden eagle, which is still found in reasonable numbers in the remoter glens. Other large birds, such as the osprey, will be seen occasionally, while the buzzard and kestrel are common practically everywhere. The rounded tops of the Grampian mountains are the habitat of the moorland birds: grouse, lapwing and curlew are common; less common, and more often heard than seen, are ptarmigan, snow bunting and dotterel.

The 'wild' animal which is most likely to be seen in these parts, apart from the ubiquitous rabbit, is the red deer. The populations of these are high, many would say too high, because their present numbers inhibit the regeneration of the native woodland. Most of the smaller animals of Britain are present. Some, such as the pine marten, are very rare elsewhere while others, like the wild cat, are unique to the Highlands.

Stac Pollaidh, Suilven and Quinag, Assynt

Assynt is remarkable for its magnificent isolated mountains of Torridonian sandstone. Ice sheets have carried away all but these relics of a once-vast continent, the rocks of which were originally formed about 800 million years ago from the sediments laid down at the mouths of great rivers, which rose in what is now Greenland. The mountains stand upon an even older 'basement' of hard, resistant, knobbly terrain formed of the ancient rock known as 'Lewisian gneiss', which was formed around 2700 million years ago and named after the island of Lewis in the Outer Hebrides where it was first described. Stac Pollaidh in the foreground, though steep and craggy, is the smallest of the mountains of Assynt. Suilven, in the middle distance, and Quinag, in the background, are grander, but each of the group has its own distinctive and fascinating shape and character.

Eaval, North Uist

The character of the landscape formed by the ancient rocks of the Lewisian gneiss, half water, half land, may be clearly seen in this view of Eaval, a small but distinctive mountain south of Loch Eport on the eastern coast of North Uist. The landmasses of the Outer Hebrides are gradually sinking beneath the ocean. This geological fact is reflected in and elaborated upon by local legends, one of which suggests that what is now the Atlantic sea-bed between the Outer Isles and St Kilda, 40 miles farther out to sea to the west, was once the hunting ground of a Hebridean princess.

East Harris

The desolate terrain of East Harris, a combination of hard, ice-worn rocks and acid, waterlogged hollows, is swept by rain and wind for a large part of the year and is almost totally bare of trees and vegetation other than the small bogland plants which decay to form acid deposits of peat. This was the land to which smallholders were forcibly removed from their traditional dwellings on the fertile western seaboard of the islands, shown opposite, during the Highland Clearances of the nineteenth century – a land where, as one Harris crofter bitterly remarked, 'beasts could not live'.

A famous taunt of Harris folk by Lewismen still runs to the effect that on Harris the stones are so close together that the noses of the sheep have to be sharpened so that they can get at the grass.

West Harris

The fertile western seaboard of the Outer Hebrides is justly famous for its miles of white shell-sand beaches, backed by fertile greenswards known as *machairs*. The view here is from Scarista, with Borve and Luskentyre behind and the Clisham, the highest mountain in Harris, in the far distance.

Cape Wrath

The furthermost north-west corner of Scotland is the appropriately named Cape Wrath, where sea cliffs of the old, hard 'foreland' of gneissic rocks rise to 135m (450ft) above the rough waters of the Atlantic Ocean.

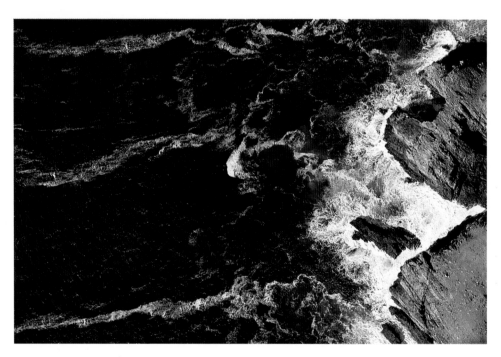

Ladhar Bheinn and Loch Hourn

The adjacent high mountains and the steep sides of Loch Hourn, formed by glacial over-deepening of a river valley which existed before the last Ice Age, make it the closest counterpart in Scotland to a Norwegian fjord. It is one of the many long, winding sea-lochs which penetrate deeply into the western coastline of the Highlands. The dramatic craggy summit of Ladhar Bheinn in the distance is formed of metamorphic rocks, younger than the ancient gneisses found mainly further north and west, but older than those of the Grampians further east, and the Cuillins to the west. The mountain has been sculpted into magnificent corries and sharp ridges by the action of ice.

Part of it has recently been purchased by the John Muir Trust, a voluntary conservation society whose aims are similar to those of the Scottish-American 'father of the conservation movement' from whom it takes its name: to preserve and restore tracts of 'wild' land, including the re-establishment of their natural forest cover, destroyed by human activity and the grazing pressure of deer and sheep over thousands of years.

Creag Meagaidh Lochaber

We are looking here south-westwards across a late-lying snow-bed on the rounded plateau-like top of Creag Meagaidh towards the distant summit of Ben Nevis, the dark crags of whose precipitous north face may be seen on the horizon at top right of the photograph. In the wild intervening country are the mountains of the Mamores.

Ben Nevis, Lochaber

The rather unexciting southern slopes of Ben Nevis, at 1343m (4406ft) Britain's highest mountain, up which it has proved possible to drive a motor car on to the summit, do not prepare us for the majestic 600m (2000ft) cliffs of the north face, a glimpse of which can be seen in this aerial view. Although 'The Ben' is mainly formed of pink granite, the cliffs and uppermost parts are formed of bedded lavas, and other volcanic rocks which were intruded when a huge block of granite foundered and collapsed into a subterranean cauldron of molten rock almost 400 million years ago.

Am Buchaille ('The Herdsman'), Staffa

The tiny volcanic 'basaltic masterpiece' of Staffa is one of the best-known islands in Europe, due more than anything to Felix Mendelssohn's famous overture 'The Hebrides', which was inspired by his visit to the island in 1829, and especially by his impressions of Fingal's Cave (named after Finn MacCumhail, the great warrior giant of Celtic mythology). The island first became known to a wider world than the inhabitants of nearby Mull, Ulva and Iona after the visit of botanist and explorer Joseph Banks in 1772 and, thereafter, those of Queen Victoria, Walter Scott, John Keats, William Wordsworth, J M Turner and Mendelssohn himself.

In Gaelic legend, Staffa is a piece of Ireland's 'Giant's Causeway', dropped by the giant; similar columnar basaltic lavas also appear in that country, in County Antrim.

Ben More, Mull

Another product of volcanic activity is Ben More, the highest summit upon the 'grate rough isle' of Mull. Ben More is here seen generating clouds, as is its wont, by the uplifting of a damp airstream, which is seldom lacking; its top is more often, however, also enveloped in them. Ben More and its surroundings, the remains of the 'Mull volcano', active 50–60 million years ago, have been described in the Geological Survey of Scotland (1924) as 'the most complicated igneous centre as yet accorded detailed examination anywhere in the world'. Its influence was widespread: swarms of 'dykes', thin vertical sheets of igneous rock which cut through the surrounding strata, radiate out from this huge centre of volcanic activity as far as the Outer Hebrides in the north-west and northern England in the east.

The Cuillins, Skye
from Plockton

The Gaelic poet Sorley MacLean's '*mur eagarra gorm*', the 'exact and serrated blue rampart' of the Cuillins is here seen across the magical waters which separate the Isle of Skye from the mainland at Plockton on Loch Carron.

The Black Cuillins, Skye
from Loch Scavaig

The splintery, ice-carved and frost-shattered peaks of the 'Black' or 'Blue' Cuillins, considered by many skilled climbers to be the most exciting mountains in Britain, are formed from coarsely crystalline volcanic rocks. They are some of the youngest of our mountains, being less than 50–60 million years old. In the centre of the photograph here is Bidein Druim nan Ramh one of the craggy summits on the great, curving sawtooth ridge which runs from the peak of Sgurr nan Gillean in the north-east to Sgurr Alasdair, the highest point (993m, 3257ft), in the south-west.

Corries of Braeriach
Cairngorms

The great corries of Braeriach (Braigh Riabhach, 'the brindled, greyish one') are dramatic examples of the classic glacial features which abound in the Cairngorms, the largest mass of really high 'arctic' land in the British Isles. Braeriach (1294m, 4248ft) forms a peninsula of the western Cairngorm plateau, joined by the rim of An Garbh Corrie, 'the great grey corrie', on the left of the photograph, to the neighbouring mountain of Carn an t-Sabhail (Cairn Toul). Together, these mountains form the south-western side of the gloomy trough of the Lairig Ghru, through which passes one of the best-known long walks in the Highlands.

The 'Old Man' of Hoy
Orkney

The Orkney Islands, separated from the Scottish mainland by the tide races of the Pentland Firth, were formed by the drowning of a faulted sandstone plateau. This was laid down as sediments some 360 million years ago in a lake basin ('Lake Orcadie'), which extended from Shetland to the Moray Firth and which lay on the surface of a now-vanished continent. The island of Hoy, in the south-west of the archipelago, is remarkable for its immense western cliffs, where the sea has penetrated natural joints in the rock to form an impressive range of erosional features, the most spectacular of these being the famous pinnacle of the 'Old Man'.

Loch Maree and Slioch

'The biggest effect man has exerted on the history of the Highlands has been in the destruction of the ancient forest – the Great Wood of Caledon. This has happened within historic time [from] AD 800 ... Even our own day cannot be exempt from this vast tale of almost wanton destruction ... Many of the priceless remnants [of the forest] were felled, mostly for ammunition boxes, and ... during Commando training. These facts should never be forgotten as one of the consequences of war...' So wrote Fraser Darling and Morton Boyd in *Natural History in the Highlands and Islands* (1964). Some of the best surviving strtetches of the old forest of Scots pine are to be found here on the south-western shores of Loch Maree. Many of these now form part of the Ben Eighe Nature Reserve, and the Nature Conservancy Council are working to rehabilitate them, successfully encouraging the regeneration of the old pines.

Woodland Plants on a Treeless Hillside Coire Dhorrcail

Plans to re-establish 'natural' forest are also under way in Knoydart, where the John Muir Trust (see also p. 22) have bought the northern slopes of Ladhar Bheinn and have begun to fence out grazing animals from some areas to allow the regeneration of woodland. Here on the lower slopes of Ladhar Bheinn, woodland wild flowers such as violets, wood anemones and wild hyacinths are still often found, indicating that these now bare hillsides were fairly recently clothed with trees.

Birch Woodland
near Loch Tummel

Birch woodland is far more extensive than pinewood in the Highlands today. In April and May the leaves are a dazzling and joyful green and the woods are suddenly filled with the song of a host of returning birds, most characteristically that of the willow warbler. Birch may be found alone as here in Daloist Birchwood, or together with pine or oak. The trees, which are relatively short-lived, tend to regenerate most readily outside the limits of the existing wood, so that birch woods are found to 'move' over a period of time.

Oak Woodland
near Loch Achray
Trossachs

The original oak forests were concentrated in Argyll, Glen Mor and on the western coasts, extending as far north as Wester Ross on the sunnier, well-drained soils of the northern shores of lochs or glens. A northerly relict of this original coverage is now found at Letterewe on the north-eastern shore of Loch Maree, as may be seen in the background of the photograph on p. 32. The oak woods are usually mixed with birch (as here), with ash, wych elm and alder, and sometimes also with hazel, rowan and bird cherry. In autumn, as in this photograph, they are a tapestry of bright, varied colour, especially in fairly open places where the woodland floor is carpeted with bracken, ferns, heather and blaeberry.

Red Deer Stag
Glencoe

A Highland landscape without deer would, despite the problems caused by their grazing pressure, be unthinkable. A delightful and accurate impression of the movement of a herd of deer across a mountainside is given by the Gaelic poet Duncan Ban Macintyre:

> Pleasant to me rising
> at morning
> to see them the horizon
> adorning.
>
> Seeing them so clear
> my simple-headed deer
> modestly appear
> in their joyousness…
>
> Walker, quick and grave,
> so elegant to move
> ahead of that great drove
> when accelerant.
>
> There's no flaw in your step,
> there's all law in your leap,
> there's no rust or sleep
> in your motion there.
>
> Lengthening your stride,
> intent on what's ahead,
> who of live or dead
> could outrace you?

(from *Moladh Beinn Dobhrainn*, 'The Praise of Ben Dorain', trans. Iain Crichton Smith)

Ancient Pinewood
Glen Barrisdale

This small wood of Scots pines is one of the scattered remnants of the Old Caledonian Forest or Great Wood of Caledon which once covered much of the Highlands. Many of the old trees are dying or already dead, and very few young pine trees or seedlings are to be found in the wood, which is therefore unlikely to survive for much longer unless the cause of this situation is established and measures taken to change it. A likely cause of the demise of the young trees is the heavy grazing pressure of red deer in the area.

Opinions on the deer population of the Highlands differ, but there is no doubt that a reduction in the numbers of deer, presently maintained at artificially high levels in the interest of deerstalking, and completely uncontrolled by any other predator (the last wolf having disappeared from Scotland in 1743) would allow native trees to return and bring new life to many desolate, bare landscapes.

Cairn Gorm
with Loch Etchachan in the distance

The summits of the high Cairngorm plateau have until recently been virtually untouched by human influence. No forest has grown here since the Ice Ages, and these granite boulders and lonely corrie lochans form part of an almost truly natural landscape. It is a land of extremes of wind, of rain and snow, and of temperature (with a mean average below freezing point, and with great fluctuations, during the course of the day, of both temperature and humidity). A harsh environment, then, and only inhabited by arctic-alpine plants and animals which have been able to adapt to its rigours.

Ptarmigan
Cairn Gorm

Ptarmigan are elusive, grouse-like birds of the high tops, associated in legend with the souls of the dead. They change colour in winter in the manner of the arctic hare, so that they are almost always beautifully camouflaged. All this particular bird had to do to completely disappear against the background of boulders and small plants was to move a few inches to one side, as may be seen from this pair of photographs. In spring the rattling call of the ptarmigan can be heard over long distances, although in summer they remain silent, nesting on the high tops to heights of over 1200m (4000ft).

The Treshnish Isles
from Calgary Bay, Mull

Like Staffa and Ulva, the table-like Treshnish Isles (shown here beyond the head of Calgary Bay on Mull) are parts of the same sheets of basaltic lava which form the western headlands of northern Mull. The largest island, in the centre of the group, is Lunga and the second most distant is the curiously shaped Bac Mor (the 'Great Hump'), known also as the Dutchman's Cap, where the 'brim' forms part of the raised beach systems of the Western Isles. Sheep, seals and seabirds are today the only inhabitants of the islands.

Puffin, Lunga

The Treshnish Isles are the home of many seabirds including members of the auk family, of which the puffin is one. Puffins find on Lunga perfect conditions in which to live, with suitable ground in which to make their burrows, interspersed with small, grassy mounds which form the focus of much summer social activity. Puffin populations have recently been severely threatened by a sudden drastic decline in the population of sand-eels, their staple diet, although at the time this photograph was taken supplies still seemed to be plentiful in the waters around Lunga.

Machair Flowers
North Uist

The *machairs* of the Western Isles are semi-natural, flower-studded grasslands established on the lime-rich white shell-sands immediately behind the dunes of the Atlantic seaboard. In spring and summer, as here, the *machairs* are covered by a profusion of wild flowers, and their colour changes as the season advances from a 'yellow' early phase through to a 'blue' phase later in the year as the different small plants come into flower in sequence. Their scent drifts offshore to be remarked from ships at sea, and flavours the milk of any cows that graze on them. The *machair* is a very beautiful, fragile environment, extremely sensitive to over-grazing and erosion, but its classic form is dependent upon the well-managed, moderate grazing pressure which was maintained by the practice of traditional 'souming' controls by the local community.

Machair Pasture
Tiree

Here the rich flora of the *machair* is seen in its early 'yellow' phase, enhanced by the golden light of the long summer evening of northern latitudes.

The Distant Past

The Ring of Brodgar is a circle-henge: a circle of standing stones within a rock-cut ditch. It is of immense size, being 125 Megalithic yards (103.6m) in diameter, and consisted originally of sixty large, thin, unshaped flagstones of which twenty-seven remain. It is believed that it defined an area within which the community enacted seasonal ceremonies – possibly involving the contents of tombs which are situated nearby. It has also been conjectured that it was a complex lunar observatory. The site is remarkable for its openness, being almost entirely surrounded by the waters of the lochs of Stenness and Harray and open to an enormous expanse of sky. It dates from the third millennium BC.

Solitary megaliths, massive standing stones, usually placed on rising ground and seen against a leaden sky, are a common sight in the Highlands and Islands of Scotland. Groups of standing stones, stone circles, henges and huge burial cairns, with slab-lined inner chambers, are also to be found, indicating that the land has supported some form of highly organized human activity for many thousands of years.

The earliest evidence of human settlement dates from the Middle Stone Age (Meso-lithic), a time when the climate was warmer than today and when dense forests, teeming with wildlife, covered the land. These people were hunters and gatherers who settled on islands or near coasts, so as to avail themselves of the plentiful supplies of fish, shellfish and birds, which the sea could provide. They lived in caves or wooden shelters; little evidence of them remains.

It was the Neolithic settlers, who arrived around the beginning of the third millennium BC, who erected the first megaliths. These were farmers who grew crops and kept animals. They brought with them skills in arts and crafts and were responsible for the first earthenware pottery. Around 2000 BC they began to raise chambered cairns as burial mounds and within 200 years had developed skills in stone-moving to the point where the erection of megaliths could begin. This type of activity suggests that times were peaceful, that there was reasonable freedom from want and that a considerable degree of social organization had developed.

From 1600 BC Bronze Age peoples were arriving from Europe, and these continued to erect megalithic structures which constitute the sole evidence of their having had any form of religious belief or practice. The purpose of henges and stone circles is a matter of conjecture, however, with the most favoured explanations being that they were connected with sun worship, or that they had some astronomical function related to the monitoring of the passage of the seasons. The latter would, of course, have been useful to an agrarian society.

The Celtic immigration into the west of Scotland, which occurred from around 700 BC, brought with it Iron Age skills and techniques. These people possessed iron tools and ploughshares and they felled forests and built homesteads in both timber and stone. They also appear to have had a requirement for military security and the first fortresses in Scotland now began to appear. There were several different types, including hillforts, duns (small stone forts) and that form which is unique to Scotland, the broch.

The Romans never occupied the Highlands of Scotland but they did conduct several military campaigns there in an attempt to subdue the native people and thus secure the northern fringe of the empire. They never succeeded in this, and it is very probable that by their activities they brought about the unification of a society of many small Celtic tribes into a single kingdom, the better to resist the foreign invader. The Romans called them *Picti*, 'painted ones'. We do not know what the Picts called themselves; in fact we know very little about them. By Roman times they occupied the whole of what is now mainland Scotland north of the Forth–Clyde isthmus as well as Orkney, Shetland and the Hebrides.

Another people of Celtic origin, the Scots, gradually became settled in part of mainland Scotland at this time. These migrated from Dalriada (northern Ireland) into the extreme south west of the Pictish territory. By AD 500 they had established a separate kingdom of Dalriada and occupied the islands of Islay, Jura, the southern part of Mull including Iona, and Kintyre and Argyll on the mainland. Their capital was at Dunadd, near Crinan, in mid-Argyll.

The kingdom of Dalriada flourished, and pressure to expand eastward into the fertile lowland valley of Scotland may well have been the factor which eventually brought the Scots into conflict with the Picts. The two kingdoms were finally united in AD 843 under the Scottish king Kenneth MacAlpin, who had connections with the royal houses of both Dalriada and Pictland. After unification the Pictish traditions became almost totally eliminated and their symbol stones (massive carved monoliths), together with some metalwork, plus archaeological evidence of duns, forts and settlements, and some burials, are the only evidence which remains of them. The obliteration of their traditions is all the more remarkable considering that the symbol stones constitute a vigorous, precise artistic symbolism and indicate the existence of a coherent system of mythology and beliefs.

The conversion of Scotland to Christianity took place during the Pictish period. St Columba (Colum Cille) came to Scotland in the mid-sixth century and persuaded the Pictish king to give him the island of Iona on which to found a monastery. He carried his mission into Pictland and in the course of the next two centuries the conversion of the whole of the mainland seems to have been accomplished. Columba's coming resulted in Iona becoming the centre of the church in Dalriada and Pictland. It became the burial place of the Scottish kings who continued to be interred there until well into the medieval period.

Carved Cross
Kilchoman, Islay

This late medieval cross at
Kilchoman on Islay, with its
biblical scenes and well-planned
interlaced trilobate foliage, is a fine
example of the Iona school of
carving. The influence of the Iona
workshop is to be found
throughout Argyll and the Western
Isles, and its spread was facilitated
by the political cohesion which
existed in the area at the time of the
Lords of the Isles, who were
patrons of the Abbey of Iona.

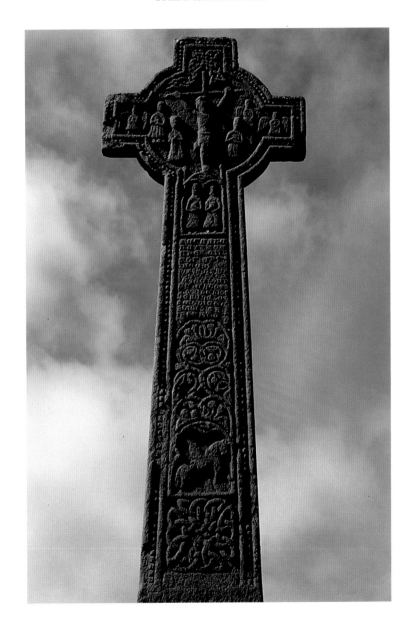

The Clava Cairns
near Inverness

There are three impressive burial cairns at Clava, situated within a wooded enclosure. All exhibit a high degree of architectural competence and the majority are surrounded by a ring of standing stones, a feature which makes the group unique in Britain. The cairn illustrated is a passage grave in which a central round burial chamber, lined and roofed with slab stones, is made accessible through a similarly constructed straight passage, aligned on a south-west axis and therefore with the mid-winter sunset. It is amongst the oldest monuments in Scotland being of the third millennium BC.

Stone Circle
Callanish, Lewis

The Callanish stone circle stands on a ridge of rock close to the shore of Loch Roag on the Atlantic coast of Lewis. It consists of a circle of standing stones at the centre of a cross formed by single lines of stones radiating to the south, east and west and an avenue (double line) of stones stretching to the north. The arrangement is unique and has baffled archaeologists, though astronomers have suggested that it may have been a calendrical computer or a lunar observatory.

This group of stones, taken with the others on the Atlantic seaboard of Scotland, points to the existence of a Neolithic people who had developed a sophisticated mathematics which was in advance of those of contemporary Mediterranean cultures. They may also have been aware of the properties of the right-angled triangle many hundreds of years before Pythagoras propounded his famous theorem.

Skara Brae
Orkney

Skara Brae was discovered in the early nineteenth century when a violent storm stripped grass and sand from a coastal location to reveal a cluster of stone houses now thought to have been occupied between 3100 and 2450 BC. Each consisted of a single large room formed by a thick dry-stone wall, roofed with timber and connected to its neighbours by narrow irregular passages topped by stone slabs, for the whole tightly knit group was subterranean. Each house had a central hearth and was equipped with stone slab furniture – large sideboard-like presses and box beds being the most remarkable. According to an HMSO book by Anna Ritchie, 'To these bare essentials the visitor's eye should add heather and furs to the beds, skin canopies spanning the bed-posts, pottery jars to the dresser, flame to the hearth, dried meats and fish hanging from the rafters...' to imagine what the dwellings must have been like at the time of their occupation.

Cup-and-Ring-Marked
Rock, Cairnbaan

Outcrops of rock with inscribed cup-and-ring markings are to be found in several places in the Highlands, particularly in Argyll. Similar patterns have also been cut into standing stones, cist covers and stones which form parts of tombs. They date from the second millennium BC and are amongst the most mysterious evidence left to us of Neolithic culture. It has been suggested that they are related to the labyrinth design which was widespread throughout the Mediterranean world at the time or that they are formalized conceptions of a source of light such as the sun. Another possibility is that they are star maps, with the number of rings surrounding each cup being indicative of brightness.

Sgurr of Eigg
from Muck

The Sgurr of the island of Eigg, 'a ship of black rock whose prow is the mighty Sgurr rock', forms the skyline in this photograph. One of the most distinctive features of the Inner Hebrides, it was fortified by the Picts in the early years of the first millennium AD and was probably also used by the Scots. At this time, when travel overland was difficult and hazardous, the Western Isles were a meeting place for travellers, being situated on the sea paths of the Celtic world.

Dun Telve Broch
Glenelg

The broch is a peculiarly Scottish type of fortified homestead which is thought to have been developed by the northern prehistoric Picts and used by them in the first century BC and the first and second centuries AD. They are circular in plan with high dry-stone walls of great thickness containing mural chambers and stairs. There were no external openings except the tiny well-protected entrance, and the quality of the masonry was very fine, especially on the exterior where the joints were sufficiently thin and the wall surfaces so smooth as to make climbing impossible. The distinctive 'cooling-tower' profiles of the exteriors would also have made the scaling of the walls extremely difficult. Most brochs are situated in fertile valleys and are not provided with a water source. It therefore seems likely that they were used as temporary shelters in response to short-duration raids.

Picardy Stone
Insch, Gordon

The most intriguing legacy of the Picts is the series of symbol stones which occur throughout their territory from Shetland in the north to Fife in the south. The inscriptions on these, which are carved into the rough undressed slabs with masterly control of line, indicate that the Picts had a coherent language of symbolism. The photograph shows one of the fourteen pagan symbols which the Picts used – a double disc and Z-rod with ornate flame-like terminals. The stone dates from the sixth or seventh century AD. The meanings of these symbols were lost when the whole culture of Pictland was submerged beneath that of the Scots from Dalriada.

Dunadd

The Scots from northern Ireland had been migrating into the south-western fringes of Pictland for many years before the seat of the principality of Dalriada was moved into what is now Argyll in about AD 500. Dunadd fort, near Kilmartin and Crinan, was the capital of Dalriada and was evidently a place of ritual significance. It is thought that a footprint and a bowl-shaped depression, which are carved into the summit rock, were used in the inauguration ceremonies of the Scottish kings.

The Scots were a Celtic people who were steeped in the Gaelic traditions of Ireland. They introduced them into what was to become Scotland, where they were to survive in the Highlands and Islands for many hundreds of years following the unification of Dalriada and Pictland. These traditions may still be considered to be alive, in some small degree, in the present day.

St Columba's Bay, Iona

In AD 563 Colum Cille, a member of an Irish royal house, embraced the religious life and travelled to Pictland where he established a Christian foundation on the island of Iona, off the south-western tip of Mull. Its location was highly significant, being on the border of Dalriada and the Pictish territories. Over the course of the succeeding centuries, first St Columba, as Colum Cille is now remembered, and then his followers converted both the Picts and the Scots to Christianity and thus helped to bring about that commonality of thought which made possible their later unification.

Iona became a religious focal point of the Celtic world. Its influence spread to every part of the Highlands and Islands and it was instrumental in shaping a way of life which was to last for many centuries.

The photograph depicts Port na Curiach, St Columba's Bay, where the saint is said to have first landed following his voyage from Ulster.

St Martin's Cross and the Abbey of Iona

The present building at Iona is a much-restored survival of the Benedictine abbey which was built there in the twelfth century, probably at the behest of Queen Margaret Canmore. Its foundation brought to a close a period of decline in the fortunes of Iona which had been caused by repeated Viking raids and subsequent Norse occupation beginning in the mid-eighth century. St Martin's Cross, in the foreground, is a Celtic ringed-cross attributed to the eighth century and, if this is correct, it is a survivor from the Columban foundation. It may however have been made in the medieval period when, under the patronage of the Lords of the Isles, Iona became a centre of stone carving. Only three crosses of note remain on Iona today. Over three hundred and sixty were cast into the sea in 1561 by zealots of the Scottish Reformation.

Kildalton Cross
Islay

The eighth-century ringed-cross at Kildalton is an outstanding example of a school of Celtic monumental sculpture. It was fashioned from a single slab of epidiorite and its overall form and boldly carved relief are the work of a consummate artist in stone. Sun symbols, reinterpreted in the context of Christianity, are an important feature of such crosses. The 'braid' motifs had important symbolic meanings, variously interpreted as the bonds of mortality, of human inadequacy and sin, or as the vitalizing powers of the Resurrection.

The Garvellachs
Firth of Lorne

The Garvellachs, or 'Isles of the Sea', are a small group of islands which lie in the Firth of Lorne between Mull and Argyll. The Celtic monastic system encouraged monks to seek occasional retreat in solitary places, and isolated islands were a favourite choice. A monastery was founded on one of the Garvellachs, Eileach an Naoimh, in the sixth century AD by St Brendan of Clonfert in western Ireland. This would have been a timber structure and nothing of it remains, but the masonry walls of later monastic buildings, probably of the ninth century, with their adjoining herb garden and burial ground, suggest that a community of moderate size once occupied this lonely place. It has been suggested that Eileach an Naoimh is the location of 'Hinba', the island monastery to which St Columba used to withdraw for contemplation. It is also, reputedly, the burial place of Eithne, the mother of St Columba.

Ardchattan Priory

The Valliscaulian priory at
Ardchattan on Loch Etive was
begun in the thirteenth century,
during the period of the Lordship
of the Isles, at a time when many
similar foundations were being
established in the Western Isles
under the patronage of the major
families of the area. A mansion
house of much later date now
occupies much of the site of the
priory but the original
arrangements can still be
appreciated. One of the main
features of interest at Ardchattan
today is the collection of carved
stones, some of which are from the
early Christian period (see p. 1).

Dunkeld Cathedral

For a short period from the mid-eighth to the mid-ninth centuries Dunkeld was the spiritual capital of Scotland. Dalriada and Pictland had been united under Kenneth MacAlpin in AD 843 and the seat of government was moved from Dunadd to Scone to render it more secure from Viking attack. The Iona community, which had been repeatedly sacked by the Vikings during the eighth century, became dispersed and the relics of St Columba were divided between a new monastery at Kells in Ireland and a newly created Scottish abbey at Dunkeld. Such had been the unifying effect of Columba's mission that the Scottish king was reluctant to allow his relics to pass out of the nation. Where the saint's relics lay, there was his church and there also was the spiritual heart of Scotland.

The photograph shows a window in the ruined nave of Dunkeld Cathedral. This building is of a much later period, having been begun in the fifteenth century. It is regarded as a fine example of Scottish medieval Gothic architecture.

The Time of the Clans

Lagavulin Bay
from Dunyvaig Castle Islay

Following the union of Scots and Picts in the ninth century the centre of Gaelic power in Scotland moved eastward to the region of Perth and Dunkeld, leaving the Western Isles at its fringe. These were under Norse rule by this time, but they were gradually won back for Gaeldom over the next five hundred years. The process was begun in the twelfth century under Somerled Macgillebrigte (part Norse, part Gael) whose family, the House of Somerled, became the many branched Clan Donald (MacDonald), the hereditary Lords of the Isles.

The Lordship of the Isles depended on sea power. Somerled had defeated the Norsemen in sea battles with a fleet of fifty-eight *naibheag* ('little ships'), which were specifically constructed to counter the Viking longships. These were berthed during the winter in Lagavulin Bay on Islay, and Dunyvaig Castle was built for their protection.

Present-day Scotland, which may be thought of as that part of the British Isles lying north of the Cheviot Hills, came into being as a political entity around the end of the first millennium AD. After the fusion of Scots and Picts under Kenneth MacAlpin in AD 843, the Canmore dynasty of monarchs imposed feudalism on the young nation in the eleventh century and extended its boundaries southwards to more or less the position of the present-day border between Scotland and England.

Feudalism is a system of government which is closely tied to the land. All land is deemed to be royal land but the king grants tenancies (fiefdoms) to his mightiest subjects, his nobles, who in return owe him a duty of military service and support. The noble could expect a title to an area of land which was large enough to generate the income required to pay for his contribution to the royal military machine – a castle, arms, armour – and to sustain a comfortable standard of living. With his feudal title the noble was given the opportunity to found a dynasty, because inheritance of the land and its privileges came under the rule of primogeniture. He also gained overlordship of the people who occupied the land; they became his serfs and were required to turn out and form the ranks in his army. Almost invariably the new feudal charters were given to Norman incomers, recruited in England and induced to come to Scotland by the promise of land and power. The process has been called the 'Normanization' of Scotland.

In the face of the military might of the crown, the Lowlands of Scotland had little choice but to acquiesce to the imposition of feudalism. In the Highlands and Islands resistance proved to be more effective probably due to the reluctance of the new Norman ruling class to venture into the gloomy, roadless vastness of the Highland areas. The feudal system was in fact abhorrent to the peoples of Gaeldom, where a tribal organization was still in existence until medieval times. This allowed no private ownership of land, which was the property of the tribe. The chiefs held their land in trust for the tribe and were appointed under the Celtic law of tanistry. Although the office was hereditary it did not pass automatically to the eldest son; the chief selected his successor from amongst the oldest and wisest men of his own family and the senior members of the tribe had to approve the choice. Rule by minors or by people who were manifestly unsuitable, one of the curses of feudalism, was therefore avoided. The original Celtic tribes, although aristocratic, allowed all members some say in their government. Any person could make his views known and chiefs who abused their position could be removed. The link of kinship resulted in a high degree of mutual respect betwen the different levels of rank within the tribe and the men of lowest rank were not treated as livestock to be acquired or disposed of with land, as they frequently were under feudalism.

The Scottish clans had their roots in the tribal structures of Celtic society. The clans whose names survive today were mostly founded in the twelfth and thirteenth centuries and were at the height of their influence and power in the fifteenth century.

Somerled, first Lord of the Isles, may be regarded as the first clan chief. He resisted attempts by the Scottish king to impose feudalism and the rule of succession by primogeniture on the Western Islands. Together with other Celtic chiefs, he attempted to halt the spread of Anglo-Norman ideas and the displacement of the Gaelic language in Scotland, but he was murdered in 1164 while campaigning on mainland Scotland for this cause. Somerled is remembered in a magical and quintessentially Gaelic song to the apple tree (*'Craoth nan Ubhal'*):

> O apple tree, may God be with you,
> may the moon and the sun be with you,
> may the wind of the east and the west be with you,
> may the great Creator of the elements be with you
> may all that ever came be with you,
> may great Somerled and his band be with you.

> (*Carmina Gadelica*)

Somerled's death was a turning point in the fortunes of the Highlands. Resistance to feudalism crumbled and all prospect of re-establishing Celtic traditions over the whole of Scotland disappeared. The Highlands were never really fully converted to feudalism however and the old Celtic traditions retained much of their vitality. Thus was born the divison of Scotland into the feudal Lowlands and the Celtic Highlands, a split which exists in some measure to the present day.

The 'Lordship of the Isles' continued after Somerled and was centred on the island of Islay, which had been Somerled's principal base. The area over which it claimed juris-

Council Isle
Loch Finlaggan, Islay

The domain of the Lordship of the Isles was to include the whole of the Hebrides and large areas of mainland Scotland particularly on the western seaboard. In the fourteenth century it was virtually a separate kingdom and had administrative headquarters at Loch Finlaggan on the island of Islay. Here the Lords were advised on Hebridean affairs by the Council of the Isles, a body of fourteen clan chiefs, and the Lord himself had his principal residence. This was a typical medieval establishment with a great hall, chapel, guest house and administrative offices. It was not fortified which gives an indication of the security of the rule. As the photograph shows, little now remains of the place which was once the capital of the Hebrides.

diction steadily increased from Somerled's time until by the fifteenth century it included all of the Western Isles, the Atlantic seaboard of mainland Scotland and areas as far east as Ross and Inverness-shire. Within this region the Lords ruled unchallenged: they could field thousands of fighting men, commanded hundreds of fighting ships and negotiated agreements with France, England, Ireland and Scotland. They were masters of what was virtually a kingdom within a kingdom, but their rule was tempered by advice from the Council of the Isles, a group of fourteen chiefs which met on the 'Council Isles' on Loch Finlaggan on Islay. In the thirteenth and fourteenth centuries, this was, in effect, the capital of the Hebrides and was a centre of wise government which brought a period of peace and prosperity to the Highlands and Islands.

It was destined not to last because the Lordship came under constant pressure from the kings of Scotland to adopt feudal principles. Gradually the Lords themselves and the chiefs of the vassal clans were persuaded to hold their lands by feudal charter in their own names, contrary to the Celtic prohibition on private land ownership, and their titles came also to be inherited according to the rule of primogeniture. As feudalism progressed through the Highlands, wise counsel deserted the chiefs and they became warlords rather than sensible administrators. The end came in 1462 when, John, Lord of the Isles, made a treaty with Edward IV of England to dismember Scotland. England would have taken the Lowlands and John's share was to have been the Highlands and Islands. It was the Scottish crown and the idea of a unified, feudal Scotland which were to survive, however, and the Lordship of the Isles which was to be abolished by the feudal Scottish monarchy. This happened finally in 1493, when the lands of the Lordship were declared forfeit by the Scottish Parliament, and it brought to a close one of the most sustained periods of good government which the Highlands were ever to see. It was followed by three centuries of feuding and strife, known as the *Linn nan Creach*, or 'Age of Forays', as the clan chiefs, now released from the restraining influence of the Council of the Isles and freed by feudalism from the constraints imposed by the Celtic system of rule by consent, adopted war and violence as the means by which affairs were conducted.

The Celtic feudalism, as it has been called, which now became the background to the Highland way of life, was a mixture of Celtic custom and Anglo-Norman feudalism. Legally, it was in fact little different from the version of feudalism practised in lowland Britain, but tradition died hard in the Highlands and the relationship between the clan chiefs and their clansmen was different to that which existed between Lowland feudal lords and their tenants. The clan was a family affair; most members had or claimed a blood tie to the chief and gave him unwavering loyalty. They recognized no higher authority, not even that of the king. Within the roadless tracts of the Highlands the chiefs were the law and sat in judgement upon their clansmen.

Many clan chiefs were very well travelled, having attended universities at Edinburgh, Glasgow, Rome or Paris. They were intensely proud individuals who placed great store by honourable behaviour, as they defined it, and who were ever ready to defend their own honour with the sword. They measured their wealth and power by the number of armed men whom they could muster and the number of cattle in their glens.

Clansmen were experienced fighters with sword and dirk (dagger). In times of peace they were herdsmen, raising black cattle, goats and sheep and also practising limited cultivation of the thin acid soils. They made little use of money and their fighting skills were highly developed, no doubt due to the necessity for defending their flocks. Cattle raiding and blood feuds between the clans were endemic and memories were extremely long. It is small wonder that clans made effective regiments in the king's army in time of war, should their chief choose to call them out.

The Highland culture was an oral one. Except for the chief and the high-ranking members of his family there was no schooling. Ordinary clansmen had no need of it. The bardic legends, the songs and the music of the pipes provided spiritual enrichment and gave explanation of their surroundings and background. The bard and the piper were the repositories of the clan traditions and were therefore extremely important members of the community.

The Highlanders were a people who looked westward to the Celtic culture for their roots. Theirs was a way of life which was totally foreign to the Lowlander who lived in a mercantile society and who, as the ideas of the Renaissance filtered slowly northward and into Britain, considered more and more that his roots were in the Mediterranean. When the final clash between these cultures came in the eighteenth century it was to be a bloody affair and disastrous for the Highlander, who was regarded in lowland Britain with complete lack of sympathy as a primitive savage.

Howmore, South Uist

The churches of St Mary and St Columba at Howmore, on the west coast of South Uist, now lie in ruins, like the headquarters of the Lords of the Isles at Finlaggan on Islay. South Uist was notable as a centre of learning during the time of the Lordship, when the western seaboard of Scotland was in direct and regular contact, both culturally and commercially, with the rest of Europe. At the end of the seventeenth century, when Martin Martin visited the Western Isles (and gave us one of the earliest written accounts of the area, *A Description of the Western Islands of Scotland*, published in 1703), this legacy of Gaelic scholarship was still in evidence in South Uist.

Inverlochy Castle Fort William

Inverlochy Castle, which dates from the thirteenth century, was destined to witness several episodes in the bloody history of clan feuding in the Highlands following the forfeiture of the Lordship in 1493. There were several battles at Inverlochy, one of which, fought in 1645, is the subject of the famous poem by the Gaelic poet Ian Lom (John MacDonald), in which he exults with 'a controlled venom, an unholy exultation' over the defeat of the Campbells, the enemies of his clan:

Alisdair, son of handsome Colla,
Skilled hand at clearing castles,
You put to flight the Lowland
    pale-faces
What kale they had taken came
    out again.

This battle was part of a wider conflict between the Parliamentarians and the Royalists during the reign of Charles I. The Campbells were on the side of the Parliamentarians and were ultimately victorious. They were destined to take ample revenge on the MacDonalds for their defeat at Inverlochy.

Castle Stalker
Appin

Castle Stalker was one of the strongholds of the Stewarts of Appin, a branch of the royal House of Stuart. The first building on this site, which is called Cormorant Rock, was erected during the thirteenth century as a seat for royal hunting and fowling expeditions, and it has been said that it was from here that James IV ordered the forfeiture of the Lordship of the Isles in 1493. The castle seen today dates from the mid-sixteenth century and has been extensively restored in recent years.

Kildrummy Castle
Gordon

Kildrummy is an example of a fortress-residence built by a rich feudal lord to 'declare his social prestige and flaunt his wealth'. It incorporates features which are typical of the age of castle building which occurred in thirteenth-century Europe and it played a key role in the imposition of feudalism on the eastern Highlands of Scotland. It also saw some action in the Wars of Independence between Scotland and England and, towards the end of its life, served as the headquarters of the Earl of Mar during the ill-fated Jacobite rising of 1715. It was besieged many times and on one occasion, during the Wars of Independence, fell to the English as a consequence of treachery by one of the castle blacksmiths, who was rewarded, it is said, by having the gold he was promised poured liquid down his throat.

The photograph shows the interior of the courtyard. The three lancet windows of the chapel are prominent and the site of the great hall is on the left.

Balvenie Castle
Dufftown

Balvenie Castle, like Kildrummy, was built in the thirteenth century at the time of the feudalization of the eastern Highlands. Originally it was a castle of enclosure, more-or-less rectangular in plan, and parts of the original curtain wall can be seen in the photograph on the extreme right and forming the lower part of the front, to the left of the entrance close. The range in the foreground, with the large windows and round tower, was added in the sixteenth century. This is a spacious set of apartments, designed in the manner of palace architecture of the Scottish Renaissance. On the first floor it consists of a hall, outer chamber and inner chamber, the latter being in the round tower. A similar suite of rooms is provided on the second floor and these may have been occupied by Mary, Queen of Scots, when she visited the castle in 1562.

Dunottar Castle
Stonehaven

Dunottar was one of the most important feudal castles in Scotland, being the residence of the 'Great Marischal', one of the principal offices of state introduced under feudalism. The earliest extant building is the fourteenth-century tower-house in the foreground of the photograph. A complete mansion house was added subsequently (the courtyard block furthest from the camera), with a great hall, lord's private chambers, chapel and seven sets of lodgings for guests and retainers. The arrangement is English in character being similar to the country houses of the Elizabethan gentry.

Dunottar is a Lowland rather than a Highland establishment, but its occupants were mostly Royalists and Jacobites, and therefore had some affinity with Highland traditions. It has featured in many of the dramatic events of Scottish history, such as the occasion in 1652 when the Scottish regalia were saved from capture by Cromwellian forces by being lowered over the cliff and hidden in a nearby church.

Edzell Castle

Edzell Castle lies on the south-eastern fringe of the Highlands and is surrounded by fertile farmland. The original fifteenth-century building was the tower-house seen on the left of the photograph, which was designed largely with security in mind. The accommodation was greatly extended in the sixteenth century by the additions seen to its right, and the building was given an outward aspect by the enlargement of the windows. At this time a walled garden containing a formal parterre was added to produce a house in which a cultivated and prosperous family could live in comfort and style.

Edzell Castle

The walled garden at Edzell is perhaps its most notable feature, with the decorative treatment of the inside face of the wall being of particular interest. This has been divided into compartments with niches for busts, recesses for flowers and with sculptured panels. There are twenty-two of the latter, which depict the planetary deities, the liberal arts and the cardinal virtues. Prudentia, illustrated in the photograph, looks at her face in a mirror, self-knowledge being the foundation of prudence.

Craigievar Castle
Lumphanan

Craigievar Castle was completed in 1626 and is more a country house than a castle. Originally it had an attached *barmkin* (a walled courtyard sheltering the stables, byre, dairy-house and other offices). This was a feature of most ancient Scottish tower-houses but at Craigievar it was subsequently swept away. The archaeological dig in the foreground of the picture was carried out to trace the line of its foundations.

Craigievar was built for 'Danzig Willie', an Aberdeenshire merchant who had made a fortune trading in the Baltic. In the words of W D Simpson in his account of the building, 'Danzig Willie [was] a specimen of the new type of Scottish laird who, turning his back on the old wild life of feudal strut and strife, enters the honourable path of commerce, marries a bourgeois wife, and finishes up by leaving to his descendants, and to Scotland, the most cultured, scholarly and refined of all her many castles.' The arrangement of the building is based on that of the traditional tower-house but the features are refined to produce a composition of some architectural distinction.

Crathes Castle
Banchory

Crathes, like Craigievar, is an example of a late Scottish tower-house whose features evolved from those of a more traditional building type. In the original fortress tower-houses the lower walls were deliberately plain and had small window openings for reasons of security. Active defence was confined to the upper levels where parapets with machicolations were provided. The core of the structure was a single large space, the great hall, and smaller rooms were located above, often in corbelled turrets and towers. Steeply pitched roofs were used to throw off rain and snow. For purely functional reasons these traditional buildings were therefore tall with plain walls, increasing in complexity towards the top. In castles like Crathes, which had no military function, this basic form was developed into an architectural style which is distinctively Scottish. Known as 'Scots Baronial', it was to affect all subsequent ages of Scottish architecture, including Classical architecture.

The Jacobite Risings

Kintail
*with Skye and the Sound
of Sleat in the background*

Prince Charles Edward Stuart traversed these ranges during his flight from the Hanoverian forces after the Battle of Culloden, the final defeat of the Jacobites. He was eventually taken off from Loch nan Uamh, near Arisaig, by a French armed brig, on which he returned to France to a life of frustration and rejection by the courts of Europe and eventually to a dissolute old age. The five months 'in the heather' were perhaps the noblest period of his life: 'Show me a king or prince in Europe cou'd have borne the like, or the tenth part of it' wrote MacDonald of Lochgarry. By his actions during the flight, Charles Edward gave to the world one of the great stories of romantic endeavour and thus secured his own immortality.

Speed, bonnie boat, like a bird on the wing,
'Onward' the sailors' cry,
Carry the lad that is born to be king
Over the sea to Skye.

('Skye Boat Song')

The 'lad that is born to be king' was Charles Edward Stuart, 'Bonnie Prince Charlie', who was the grandson of James VII of Scotland & II of England, the last Stuart king of Britain and Ireland. James was deposed in the 'Glorious Revolution' of 1688, and thus was precipitated the Jacobite Movement, an organization which was dedicated to the restoration of the Stuart dynasty. The exiled Court became established in France from where it sought support from the European powers which were hostile to England. The 'Skye Boat Song' describes an episode in Charles Edward's flight following the Battle of Culloden. This was the conclusion of the Jacobite war of 1745–6, which was the fourth occasion that an armed attempt at restoration had been mustered in the Highlands of Scotland. This mountainous region was the obvious location in Britain in which to begin any military campaign against the government: the country was wild and could not be effectively policed, many Highland people were sympathetic to the Stuart cause, and the clan system could furnish a ready-made army.

The first uprising occurred in 1689 and resulted in an early Jacobite victory at the Battle of Killiecrankie. The campaign was badly organized, however, and easily overcome. A projected rising in 1708 failed to materialize on British soil and the two sides did not come to physical blows again until 1715. On both these occasions, success should have been possible due to the extreme unpopularity of the government as a consequence of the Act of Union (of the parliaments of Scotland and England) of 1707. On both occasions, however, the cause was bedevilled by poor leadership and lack of co-ordination between British Jacobites and the foreign powers on which they depended for financial support. An attempted rising in 1719, in which a small force of Spanish troops was landed in Kintail, also ended in failure. All of these were, however, to be but a prelude to the one rising which almost did succeed, 'the '45'.

The expedition of 1745–6 – the *Bhliadhna Thearlaich* ('Charlie's Year') of the Gaelic world – which was to excite the imaginations of the romantic chroniclers of the nineteenth century, was nevertheless destined to be the final episode in the Jacobite saga. At the outset, however, hopes were high. At last the cause had a dynamic and charismatic figurehead in the 'Bonnie Prince' and an able military leader in Lord George Murray.

The rising began in July 1745 when Charles Edward Stuart landed on the shore of Loch nan Uamh, between Arisaig and Moidart on the west coast of Scotland. The Jacobite standard was raised at Glenfinnan and a group of clans joined the Prince in a march south, firstly to Edinburgh and then, following the Battle of Prestonpans, into England. At Derby, just one hundred miles short of London, the leaders suffered a loss of nerve and at a meeting of the Jacobite Council of War the decision was taken, against the wishes of Charles Edward, to withdraw again to Scotland. There seems little doubt that this was the most fateful decision ever taken by a Jacobite group. Opinions of historians differ, but it may be argued that had they continued south from Derby the Jacobites would have succeeded in occupying London. There is no telling what the outcome might then have been, for some consider it likely that at this stage substantial support would have been forthcoming from both France and the English Jacobites.

The return northwards was orderly: a skirmish occurred at Penrith, which may have been the last battle ever fought in England, and the Jacobites were victorious over government forces at Falkirk in central Scotland. Still the retreat continued, however, and the final battle was fought on Culloden Moor in April 1746. Although the Jacobites were defeated in this, the battle was by no means a rout and was not regarded at the time as the end of the campaign. As on previous occasions, however, the clans failed to re-muster and the Jacobites were destined never again to challenge the ruling oligarchy.

Culloden was the last battle fought on British soil. It brought to an end the hopes of the Stuart dynasty of ever regaining the British crown and its aftermath was remarkable for two things: the flight of Charles Edward and the ferocity of the behaviour of the government troops under the Duke of ('Butcher') Cumberland, the younger son of George II.

Whatever the final judgement on what Derick Thomson, professor of Celtic at Glasgow University, has referred to as 'the dynastic struggles of Scoto-English and German royalty [which] were ... a pathetic source of disunity in Gaelic Scotland', the flight of Prince Charles Edward was a truly remarkable adventure. He travelled southwards from

Inverness by way of the Great Glen to Borrodale near Arisaig whence a hazardous sea voyage was made in a small boat to the Outer Hebrides. There, he lived the life of a fugitive, always on the move, spending nights in the open or in small bothies, and travelling almost the entire length of that chain of islands from Stornoway to Lochboisdale, mostly in small boats among the islets and inlets of the extremely inhospitable east coast. Finally, in the company of the remarkable Flora MacDonald, and disguised as her woman servant, he escaped to the Isle of Skye, and then back to the mainland, where his wanderings continued in the wild mountain country of the western Highlands until, in late September, he was taken off by a French brig from the very spot near Arisaig where he had first landed fourteen months before. Throughout most of this period he was pursued closely by Hanoverian forces. The Hebridean seas were full of hostile ships and small boats searched for the Prince along the coastline and in the inlets. He was almost captured on several occasions and was totally dependent on his supporters, followers and well-wishers who sheltered him throughout. Most of those who helped him, including Flora MacDonald, were subsequently arrested, usually within days of having delivered him on to the next group who were to guide him, so hot was the pursuit, and many were punished. It is a tribute to the strength of the Highland code of honour that although many hundreds of people must have known of his whereabouts, none betrayed him for the £30,000, indeed a prince's ransom in those days, which the government offered for his capture.

The period of repression which followed Culloden was one in which the Hanoverian regime attempted to completely obliterate the Highland way of life, in order that this particular threat to their succession should never recur. Although contemporary and later accounts inevitably became elaborated and exaggerated, it seems true nevertheless that very many acts of barbarity were committed by the Hanoverian army upon the population of the Highlands: people were driven from their homes and fugitives were hunted and killed in brutal fashion. This was by all accounts in complete contrast to the behaviour of the Highland army, which throughout the Jacobite wars treated prisoners and enemy wounded with magnanimity.

The events of the troubled years in the Highlands between the battles of Killiecrankie and Culloden have passed into Highland folk memory. Calum MacLean, twentieth-century Highlander and Gaelic scholar, who made the collection and recording of the stories and tales of the Gaelic oral tradition his life's work, related the incidents of 'the '45' as though they were part of living memory: there is scarcely a page in his book *The Highlands*, first published in 1959, on which some reference to the Jacobite wars is not made. The events were clearly seen as a very significant part of Highland history, albeit a negative one from the Gaelic standpoint. The departure of Prince Charles Edward was a turning point for Gaeldom. Symbolically if not literally it marked a significant victory of rationalism and mercantilism over its ancient culture.

Loch Lomond

O Ye'll tak' the high road,
And I'll tak' the low road,
And I'll be in Scotland afore ye,
For me and my true love will
    never meet again
On the bonnie bonnie banks o'
    Loch Lomond.

This well-known Scottish song is a Jacobite lament. Various opinions exist on the exact meaning of these lines but in one version the words are attributed to a prisoner on one of the fever-ridden hulks moored in the Thames estuary near London after the '45: the 'high-road' back to Scotland led by way of the scaffold and the 'low road' was that taken by those who succumbed to disease.

Kilchurn Castle
Loch Awe

Kilchurn Castle was one of the strongholds in the 1690s of Sir John Campbell, Earl of Breadalbane. Although he had Jacobite sympathies, he nevertheless offered himself, early in the days of the new dynasty, to King William as the only man who could 'bring in' the Jacobite clan chiefs. These he met at Achallader in the summer of 1691 and, through argument and the offer of a cash indemnity, negotiated a temporary peace. McIain, chief of the Glencoe MacDonalds, who was to die eight months later in the Massacre of Glencoe, was not convinced, saying prophetically that he had no trust in someone who was 'Willie's man in Edinburgh and Jamie's in the Highlands'. Breadalbane, who was implicated in the Massacre, did not succeed in becoming the head of Clan Campbell, despite all his machinations. He died in his bed, however, at the age of eighty.

Monument to Duncan Ban Macintyre
from Kilchurn Castle

Allegiances were often complex and divided during the Jacobite risings, and not only for those of elevated social rank. One of those who fought briefly and unenthusiastically for the Hanoverian side in 1746, despite some Jacobite leanings, was the Gaelic poet Duncan Ban Macintyre (Donnchadh Bàn Mac an t-Saoir). His monument can just be seen on a hillock below the horizon, looking southward from Kilchurn. He is best known for his sensitive and closely observed depictions of nature. The greatest of these, from 'The Praise of Ben Dorain', is the tribute to the deer which begins:

> Pleasant to me rising
> at morning
> to see them the horizon
> adorning...

This poem (from which a longer quotation appears on p. 30), has been described by Derick Thomson in *An Introduction to Gaelic Poetry* as '[in some ways] the foremost praise song in Gaelic – an ironic reflection, when we consider the generations of bards trained to praise human chiefs and patrons'.

Buchaille Etive Mor
Glencoe

Buchaille Etive Mor stands at the entrance to Glencoe on the fringes of the 'wilderness' of Rannoch Moor. It was believed in the Highlands that all men of Glencoe were poets from birth and that the paternity of any who could not demonstrate this was in doubt. The land here is amongst the least fertile in the Highlands and perhaps for this reason the MacDonalds of Glencoe 'were by nature rievers and cattle lifters'. Many clans, not least the neighbouring Campbells, had scores to settle with them, and the opportunity was taken when by the 'special command' of King William a Campbell regiment was ordered to 'fall upon the rebels, the MacDonalds of Glencoe and put all to the sword under seventy'.

Glencoe

The 'Massacre of Glencoe' occurred in the early morning of 13 February 1692. Thirty-eight persons of a small branch of the MacDonald clan, including two women, two children and the old chief, were murdered by a small party of soldiers from a Campbell regiment which had been quartered in their midst. The justification for this inhuman act, one of the foulest of the Jacobite period, was the failure of the chief, in confusing circumstances, to take the oath of allegiance to William of Orange by the prescribed date. It was intended as a warning to other recalcitrant chiefs but they were hardly likely to be intimidated by this kind of deed: to the Highlander perhaps the most serious crime involved was the violation of the sacred tradition of hospitality.

Rob Roy's Grave Balquhidder

The folk hero Rob Roy, a leading member of the oppressed clan of MacGregor, finally ended his days peacefully at Balquhidder where he was buried in 1734. Outlawed for crimes for which it was not wholly responsible (despite a certain deserved notoriety for thieving and cattle-raiding), the clan was dispossessed of its lands and even the use of the name MacGregor. Rob Roy, a well-educated and astute individual, was an able leader of his men but was caught among the intrigues of more powerful clans. He narrowly escaped transportation to penal servitude in Barbados in 1719 following his involvement in the Jacobite rising of that year, although his active participation in the cause was probably confined to the final action at Glenshiel. He is remembered as a 'Robin Hood' figure and a fitting epitaph is spoken for him by Andrew Fairservice, in Walter Scott's 'Rob Roy': 'There [are] many things ower bad for blessing, and ower gude for banning, like Rob Roy.'

Loch Katrine, Trossachs

Loch Katrine, in the Trossachs, is in the heart of 'Rob Roy country', the demesne of 'that old, proscribed, nameless, redhanded clan of the MacGregors', an area which travellers once feared to pass but is now much visited.

Eilean Donan Castle Dornie

Eilean Donan Castle was the principal Jacobite magazine during the unsuccessful rising of 1719. It was besieged and eventually blown up by the Royal Navy, forcing the Jacobites to retreat inland with meagre supplies of food and ammunition, and rendering their eventual defeat inevitable. The castle remained a total ruin until its restoration in 1912–32.

The 'Five Sisters' of Kintail

The mountains known as the 'Five Sisters' of Kintail formed the backdrop to the Battle of Glenshiel, the concluding action of the 1719 rising. The two sides here were fairly evenly matched, and the Jacobites included a small force of regular Spanish troops. The firepower of the Hanoverians was superior, however, leading to the eventual rout of their opponents. The Highlanders melted away into the hills leaving the unfortunate Spaniards to surrender. The affair ended with a touch of farce as the victors fell into confusion concerning who should pay the expenses of the Spanish prisoners. The local Hanoverian commander was instructed to obtain a signed IOU from the prisoners for the cost of their repatriation. The final solution was the retention of the Spanish commander as a hostage for their debts.

Bernera Barracks Glenelg

Bernera was one of four infantry barracks which were built after the Jacobite rising of 1715 as part of a series of measures intended to 'prevent insurrections of the Highlanders ... and to hinder rebels and attainted persons from inhabiting that part of the kingdom'. They were of limited effectiveness, being vulnerable to attack by artillery. All four fell easily to the Jacobite army in the war of 1745–6.

General Wade Plaque Weem

General George Wade was posted to Scotland in 1724 and ordered 'narrowly to inspect the present situation of the Highlanders ... in regard to the depredations said to be committed in that part of Your Majesty's dominions'. He found a population which was poor, of questionable loyalty to the Hanoverian regime and well practised in the use of arms. His reaction to this potentially unstable situation was like that of many colonial governors – repressive. He strengthened the barracks and forts and established a system of military communications amounting to two hundred and fifty miles of roads and bridges. These are his chief memorial. Another, less substantial, is the portrait to be seen on the wall of the hotel at Weem, near the 'Wade Bridge' over the Tay at Aberfeldy.

The Islands of Rhum and Eigg
from Arisaig

Prince Charles Edward Stuart landed on the Scottish mainland near Arisaig on 25 July 1745. He brought with him optimism, enthusiasm, arrogance and charisma, but no troops, arms or treasure, only seven other desperate men. By this time the fortunes of the Jacobites were at a low ebb and their only hope was a successful rising of the ready-made army of Highland clans. If such a campaign could achieve substantial gains in England there was some chance that the French aid, which was essential for a complete victory, would be forthcoming. It was a desperate gamble and it did not succeed. Charles Edward was to leave Scotland fourteen months later, never to return.

Glenfinnan Monument

The monument at Glenfinnan marks the spot where the Jacobite standard was raised at the start of the 1745 rising. There was, however, no spontaneous response from the clans. None of the principal chiefs of the northern Hebrides 'came out' and it was a pitifully small group of fewer than 1500 clansmen who stood around the Stuart standard on that July day. This set the pattern for the whole campaign in which, despite the pulling power of Charles' lineage and personality, the greatest single difficulty for the Jacobites was lack of numbers. The Highlanders were understandably reluctant to become involved in an expedition which probably stood as little chance of success as its three predecessors had done and which could cost them their children's heritage as well as their own heads.

The 'Well of the Dead' Culloden Moor

The Jacobite wars ended at Culloden, near Inverness, where approximately five thousand hungry and exhausted clansmen faced the well-directed firepower of the Hanoverian army under the Duke of Cumberland. Between twelve hundred and two thousand of them perished. The Jacobites should not have offered battle that day but their leaders had little choice because the army was disintegrating through shortages of money and supplies. The inscription on this commemorative stone reads 'Well of the Dead. Here the chief of the MacGillivrays fell'. The MacGillivrays were one of the oldest of the clans. They had fought with Somerled, the first 'Lord of the Isles', in the twelfth century, during the resistance to the imposition of feudalism on the Highlands.

Grimsay, Ronay and Eaval, North Uist
from Rossinish Benbecula

It was on Rossinish, in the foreground of the photograph, that the small boat carrying the fleeing Prince Charles Edward made landfall in the Outer Hebrides, following an extremely hazardous crossing of the Minch on the night of 26 April 1746. He was to spend the next two months in this land of loch and bog, living the life of a fugitive, and the picture which emerges of him from this period is of 'a remarkably attractive young man: sturdy and resilient, uncommonly equable in face of dire misfortune and fearful discomfort'. He was to leave the Outer Isles for the Isle of Skye in late June, in the company of Fionnghal (Flora) MacDonald, disguised as her servant, Betty Burke.

The Cuillins, Skye
from Elgol

After landing on Skye with Flora MacDonald and following a short period on Raasay, the Prince walked to Elgol from Portree, a distance of thirty miles. His guide was Captain Malcolm MacLeod and the journey, over very rough country, was made mostly by night. Between them they consumed a bottle of brandy in the course of it. Again, Charles Edward assumed the role of servant and Malcolm was much concerned that he would be recognized, declaring that he could never 'dissemble his air' and that people would not fail to 'see something about him that was not ordinary, something of the stately and grand'. From Skye, he returned to the mainland, whence he departed for France.

Fort George

Fort George, near Inverness, was built in response to the Duke of Cumberland's call for new Highland forts following the exposure of the weakness of the existing structures in the '45. It was of immense size, capable of accommodating two thousand men who could be housed in underground rooms (casements), dug into the back of the huge ramparts, in time of siege. The building work was supervised by the Adam brothers, John, Robert and James, who were to become famous for their architectural exploits elsewhere, but was already unnecessary before its completion. The Highlands had been so quelled in the aftermath of the '45 that there was never to be the threat of another rising.

Ellen's Isle, Loch Katrine Trossachs

Once the true Highlander had been safely eliminated following the '45, a romanticized version, more acceptable in the south, was created in the course of the nineteenth century. Outfitted in the manner of a Scotch trifle and with characteristics which would not offend the sensibilities of bourgeois respectability, this mythical figure became the tartan-clad hero of Queen Victoria and her entourage, and subsequently of the tourist industry. Sir Walter Scott, by means of his highly dramatic Gothic tales (albeit founded on generally accurate historical research) set against the picturesque backdrop of Highland lochs and mountains, greatly advanced this movement if he did not in fact initiate it. Ellen's Isle on Loch Katrine, in the heart of the Trossachs, features in one of his earliest productions, *The Lady of the Lake*, and such was the popularity of this poem that a hotel had to be built in Callander to accommodate the annual tide of visitors to the area.

Inversnaid Waterfall Loch Lomond

Farewell to the land where the
    clouds love to rest,
Like the shroud of the dead, on
    the mountain's cold breast;
To the cataract's roar where the
    eagles reply,
And the lake her lone bosom
    expands to the sky.

These lines head the chapter in Sir Walter Scott's *Rob Roy* in which the action moves away from the 'peculiarly rough and rugged' eastern side of Loch Lomond, 'at this time the chief seat of [Rob Roy] MacGregor and his clan', and give a flavour of the highly romantic atmosphere so beloved by his nineteenth-century readers.

After 1745

Tobermory, Mull

The building of Tobermory was begun in the 1780s to a design of the British Fisheries Society. This body was a semi-philanthropic organization set up in 1786 with the principal object of establishing fishing villages in the Highlands. Its directors, who included the Duke of Argyll, and the Earls of Breadalbane and Moray, met weekly in Waghorn's Coffee House in London. In the early years many of them made frequent visits to the Highlands but normally business was conducted there through appointed agents. The land for Tobermory was acquired, 'on advantageous terms', from the Duke of Argyll, and by the early years of the nineteenth century a prosperous town had been established.

The hundred years following the Battle of Culloden were a time in which very dramatic changes occurred in the Highlands. Some of these were the result of government policy as a deliberate attempt was made to dismantle the clan system. Three Acts of Parliament were passed, one forbidding the bearing of arms, one prohibiting the wearing of Highland dress, particularly tartan, and a third abolishing the hereditary jurisdictions of the clan chiefs in an attempt to deprive them of their influence over the Highland population. It was an inevitable reaction to the armed risings which had three times disrupted the peace of lowland Britain.

The measures adopted by the government were not all repressive and a policy for the 'improvement' of the Highlands commanded widespread support in the late eighteenth century. Highland soldiers had acquitted themselves well during the wars of American Independence and were coming to be regarded in England as valuable cannon fodder rather than potential rebels. In addition, the idea of developing the Highlands was beginning to be substituted for the lost opportunity of exploiting the American colonies. A body of 'Commissioners for the Forfeited Estates' had been set up after the '45 with the primary function of administering land which had been confiscated from owners who had supported the risings, and it was now charged with the task of promoting the economic development of this 'remote' part of Britain. Fired with enthusiasm for the ideas of the Enlightenment and the new economic doctrines of Adam Smith, the Commissioners tried to open up the area to development. Communications were improved – roads, bridges and canals were built – and various schemes, mostly associated with the traditional activities of agriculture and fishing, were promoted in an attempt to introduce industry and a cash economy. These initiatives had very limited success. A fundamental difficulty lay in the poorness of the soil, which placed a natural limit on agricultural development, and the distance of the area from potential markets, which inhibited the establishment of profitable industry or commercial fishing.

Another factor was the attitude of the Highlander himself to the so-called benefits of material progress. There were countless references at the time to the 'idleness' of the population which appeared to outsiders to suffer from permanent 'constitutional sloth'. This was because it was observed that Highlanders, once the immediate needs of their families had been satisfied, would rather sit at their doors or firesides and tell stories and sing songs, than toil to improve their material lot – an ordering of priorities which lowlanders could not understand. The gulf between Gaeldom and Anglo-Norman Britain was as deep as ever and it is small wonder that 'solutions' to the 'Highland Problem' devised by career-minded or well-intentioned civil servants in London or Edinburgh should have had limited success.

The government-led attempts to reform the economic and social structures of the Highland areas did no more than add impetus to a trend which was already becoming well established before the final defeat of Jacobitism. Since the beginning of the eighteenth century the clan chiefs and other landowners had been reorganizing their estates along lines which would yield cash rents. The traditional 'townships' – multiple-tenant communal farms – were being broken up and turned into individual smallholdings (crofts) by chiefs and other gentry whose political and social ambitions were drawing them into the ways of the landed classes of lowland Britain. This was complemented by the establishment of cash-earning activities with which crofters could supplement their incomes. By the end of the eighteenth century a kelp industry, which produced chemicals for industrial processes from seaweed, was thriving in coastal areas, and the high price of cattle in the Lowlands had resulted in the establishment of profitable cattle-droving in which huge herds were driven south for sale in lowland markets. Illicit distilling of whisky was yet another substantial prop to the growing cash economy of the Highlands at this time. These activities allowed rents to be increased and stimulated consumerism.

In the early decades of the nineteenth century disaster struck: profits from kelp and droving plummeted following the end of the Napoleonic Wars, and a series of crop failures left much of the population, which had risen by 54% between 1755 and 1831, starving and destitute. The reaction of the chiefs and landowners was mixed. Some, such as MacLeod of Dunvegan, bankrupted themselves attempting to feed their tenants, but most had by this time deliberately subordinated their personal obligations as patrons and protectors in favour of the notions of progress and economic estate management. As a result their tenants were treated as redundant livestock and large numbers of people were forcibly removed from the land in the infamous Highland Clearances. Many were transported to the British colonies so that their glens could be used for sheep farming, which did produce good cash returns, or turned into equally profitable playgrounds for the rich, in the form of deer forests and grouse moors. It was one of the most shameful episodes of

British history and ended in civil unrest and, eventually, government intervention.

The Crofting Act of 1886, which resulted from the events of the Clearances, instituted a new system of land tenure in the Highland areas. Under this, the Highlander could become a relatively independent, small tenant-farmer, the master or mistress of a croft. Most crofts were small (on average seven acres) and so crofters supplemented their income in other ways such as by inshore fishing or taking up part-time employment. Thus, a new version of the traditional way of life came into being, and crofts are now a common feature of the present-day landscape of the Highlands. They exist alongside the large estates, some of which are owned by the descendants of the clan chiefs and are still dedicated, for the most part, to grouse, deer and sheep. Sheep have had a disastrous effect on the landscape, adding their grazing pressure to that of the deer. Unlike the cattle which they replaced they did not enrich the land with their dung; instead they impoverished it by nibbling too close, thereby causing huge areas of hitherto fertile land to be covered in bracken, heather and peat. If, in the words attributed by Tacitus to the Caledonian leader Calgacus, the Romans made a wilderness and called it peace, then the Highland landowners made a desert and called it progress.

Glenfiddich Distillery Dufftown, Moray

Whisky, Scotland's national drink, is particularly associated with the Highlands and Islands but the production of it on a large scale is a comparatively recent occurrence. Traditionally the common beverage was strong ale, while the gentry preferred claret or brandy. The conversion to whisky began in the late eighteenth century when the introduction of the potato released for distilling large quantities of barley formerly required for food. It was also stimulated by the imposition of heavy excise duties on spirits which made illegal distilling an effective way of converting produce into cash for the payment of rent. The illegal trade flourished until the duty was greatly reduced by government legislation in 1822, at which time a modest registration fee for stills was also imposed. Thus began the legitimate whisky industry which was to become one of the main pillars of the modern cash-based economy of the Highlands.

The Glenfiddich Distillery at Dufftown is in one of the heartlands of the mainland industry based on the rivers Spey and Fiddich and the Livet Water.

James Logan, Cooper at Glenfiddich Distillery Dufftown, Moray

Following distillation the whisky spirit must be matured for at least three years in oak casks before it legally becomes Scotch whisky. During the maturation, the makers of the finest malt whiskies, such as Glenfiddich, use a proportion of sherry casks, seen here in the barrel store, and extend the process for considerably longer than the legal minimum requirement. The matured spirit is then mixed with spring water to reduce it to drinkable strength before being bottled.

Easdale, Lorne

Easdale is one of a number of locations in the western Highlands in which a quarrying industry flourished throughout the nineteenth century. Roofing slate was exported from here to England and America as well as to other parts of Scotland. The quarries are now closed but their gaunt remains, together with the associated piers and workers' dwellings, are part of an industrial museum and are a much-visited location on the Highland tourist trail.

Bonawe Iron Furnace Lorne

For approximately one hundred years, in the late eighteenth and early nineteenth centuries, an iron industry operated in the Highlands, though the extent to which the economy of Scotland benefited from it is debatable. The Bonawe furnace was established in 1752 by an English company and was one of several which were set up in the Argyll area under agreements negotiated with the local landowners, the Duke of Argyll, the Earl of Breadalbane and Sir Duncan Campbell, who received valuable cash income from them by the leasing of timber rights. Ore was shipped here for smelting and pig iron re-exported for further processing, the attraction of the area being the abundant supply of 'cheap' timber, which was used for the manufacture of charcoal. Iron-making ceased at Bonawe in 1876, leaving bare and desolate the once thickly wooded hills of Argyll.

Crinan Canal

The Crinan Canal, which was opened in 1801, runs between Ardrishaig and Crinan in the narrow isthmus at the north end of the Mull of Kintyre, and therefore links the Firth of Clyde with the waters of the Hebrides. Some of the great names of engineering history were involved with the undertaking: James Watt made a survey for it in 1771 and both John Rennie and Thomas Telford were actively involved in its construction. The finance was raised in London but the shareholders included many Highland landowners, who expected their estates to rise in value following its opening, and Glasgow merchants, who hoped to develop a west coast trade. Like all other large-scale works intended to 'open up' the Highlands it was not a financial success due to the 'scarcity of users', but it was of great benefit to small coastal and fishing vessels.

Neptune's Staircase Caledonian Canal Banavie

The Caledonian Canal runs from Fort William in the west to Inverness in the east in the gash across Scotland which is Glen Mor, the Great Glen. In the words of one twentieth-century economic historian, A. J. Youngson: '[it] was a failure, one of those conspicuous white elephants conceived by ambitious and ingenious engineers and enthusiastically brought to birth by misguided politicians.' And yet the intentions were laudable: after its building it was envisaged that 'the migratory state of the herring fishing would be matched by the mobility of vessels', that the shipment of grain to the Highlands would be facilitated, and that trade in timber and with the slate quarries at Easdale and Ballachulish would be stimulated. Construction began in 1803 under the direction of the engineer Thomas Telford and the estimated cost of £350,000 was modest, especially compared to the eventual expenditure of well over £1,000,000. Like its predecessor at Crinan, the Caledonian Canal never fulfilled its promise but it has nevertheless proved extremely useful to generations of small-boat users.

West Highland Railway Rannoch Moor

'A wearier looking desert man never saw' is how Robert Louis Stevenson described the Moor of Rannoch in the novel *Kidnapped*. The photograph looks north-west from just north of Rannoch Station and shows one of the most desolate stretches of the West Highland Railway. Ben Nevis is one of the snowbound peaks on the skyline.

The shareholders of the 'West Highland' who were aboard the inaugural train in 1894 must have wondered where the traffic would come from to pay their dividends, because this railway, which runs from Glasgow to Fort William, is constructed mostly through a sparsely inhabited landscape of mountains and moorland. It is still open however, providing railway travellers with one of the most spectacular journeys to be had anywhere in the world. Except on special occasions the trains are now diesel-hauled, a fact regretted by John Thomas who laments in his book on the West Highland Railway: 'No longer can a traveller stand on Rannoch platform of an evening and hear the thin whistle of a locomotive far away out on the Moor'.

Eric Ross, Signalman Blair Atholl

The photograph shows Eric Ross, signalman at Blair Atholl, on the Perth-to-Inverness stretch of the old Highland Railway, facing his gleaming levers in one of the very last mechanically worked signal boxes in the British Isles, a reminder of the golden age of railways. This railway, between Inverness and Perth, was built in the 1860s, and formed a direct link between the heart of the Highlands and Edinburgh. Inverness subsequently became the hub of the railway system in the Highlands as lines to Aberdeen, Wick and Thurso, and to the west coast at Kyle of Lochalsh, were also constructed. All of these are still open. Together with roads and steamships, the railways were an important part of the Highland transport network which made possible the very dramatic changes which occurred in the region in the nineteenth century.

Buckie, Moray Firth

'The whole coast of Scotland may be considered one continual fishery', wrote John Knox in his *View of the British Empire* in 1784. Great shoals of herring, the 'silver darlings', came down the Scottish coasts every summer, and in the nineteenth century many east coast fishing communities, such as Buckie on the Moray Firth, became prosperous herring ports. The boom lasted until the early years of the present century, after which the herring shoals disappeared.

Salmon fishing has been important in Scotland since medieval times, both for home consumption and as a valuable national export. The photograph shows the modern trap nets which are used by commercial fishermen to take fish as they migrate along the coast to the rivers. The very high value of river angling for sport in the present affluent times has kept the old conflict between coastal and upstream fishing interests very much alive.

Findochty, Moray Firth

The present village of Findochty (pronounced 'Finnechtie') was founded in 1717 and is typical of the many small fishing ports which are strung out along the south shore of the Moray Firth. It enjoyed its period of greatest prosperity in the nineteenth century – one hundred and forty boats worked out of its small harbour in 1855 – but, like most other fishing settlements on the east coast of Scotland, it suffered a decline after the First World War. A few commercial fishing boats may still be seen here today, however, sharing the haven with pleasure craft. The rows of cottages, with their gable-ends presented to the sea, form a townscape which is characteristic of this part of Scotland.

Ruined Black House Arnol, Lewis

A 'black house' (*tigh dubh*) was a long rectangular building with rounded ends and very thick walls consisting of two skins of dry-stone construction with an inner core of packed earth. The single door was the only opening and the building was without chimneys; the smoke from the central peat fire found its way out through a vent hole in the roof, which was of turf or thatch, supported on a timber structure. The floor consisted of small stones placed on end and covered with a thick layer of clay, topped with white sand. The interior was subdivided into two parts with human occupants at one end and animals at the other.

The black house was the traditional dwelling of the Islands until the mid-nineteenth century; nine were still occupied in Arnol in the 1960s. The social life in the townships of black houses was rich. In an age before 'canned' entertainment, and within living memory, neighbours would congregate around the peat fire to gossip, tell stories and sing – thus preserving Gaelic traditions which had been handed down by word of mouth from antiquity.

South Dell, Lewis

Crofting landscapes were created in the early nineteenth century when Highland landowners reorganized their estates for maximum cash income. The photograph shows a typical arrangement in which the arable land is subdivided into long narrow strips each of which is an individual croft with a croft house. Crofts were deliberately made too small to be self-sufficient so as to force crofters to supplement their incomes and thus provide cheap labour for the kelp industry and commercial fishing.

Until the 1880s, when protective legislation was introduced, many crofters were very badly treated by the landowners. One of the reasons for the perpetuation of the primitive black house was that an automatic increase in rent would follow any improvement made by the crofter. Timber was a precious commodity in this treeless land but crofters were not permitted to gather driftwood which was deemed to belong to the landowner; it was not unknown for estate agents to make raids into crofters' houses for the purpose of confiscating any found to have been collected.

AFTER 1745

White House
Howmore, South Uist

'White houses' (*tighean geala*), similar in form to black houses but with lime-mortared walls, chimneys and windows, were introduced into the Highlands in the 1850s. Some are still occupied in the Outer Hebrides, having been adapted to provide standards of comfort which are acceptable in the present day.

Elphin, Assynt
with Suilven in the background

The successor to the 'black' and 'white' houses of the early days of crofting was the two-storey cottage with walls of stone or brick masonry, a slatted or corrugated iron roof and dormer windows. Normally the walls were harled (rendered) and finished with limewash. This type of building is still ubiquitous in the Highlands. Another version, in which the walls as well as the roof are covered with corrugated iron, is also seen in the photograph.

Peat Cuttings
The 'String Road'
Lewis

Peat is still cut as the normal fuel throughout the Hebrides and on many parts of the western seaboard of the Highlands. The peats are cut on the moorlands in the summer months and, following a number of stages of drying, are transported to crofts and town houses where they are built into stacks for the winter. Here on the 'String Road' in Lewis the inhabitants of Stornoway can be found attending to their peats during the long summer evenings which occur in these northern latitudes. The huts at the cuttings are successors to the 'shielings' which were used in a bygone age when the animals were taken to the summer pastures.

Peat Stack
Arnol, Lewis

By late summer large peat stacks are found at the side of every house. In the old days, the height of the smoke base in a black house depended on the type of peat. The blackest peat, which was cut from the bottom of the peat bank, gave the most heat and least smoke when dried. A newly lit fire was very smoky because

Blathaichidh an caoran dubh
  e fhein,
ma's blathaich e duin' eile.

(The black peat will warm
  itself
before it warms anybody else)

Dunrobin Castle
Golspie

Dunrobin Castle, which was built in 1835–50, is the seat of the Duke of Sutherland. The infamous Clearances which were effected on behalf of the Countess of Sutherland between 1807 and 1820, displacing the crofting population of the estate from their glens to poorer land on the coasts, were one of the most inhumane episodes in Scottish history. They were by no means unique in the Highlands, however.

The Highland Clearances were a response to the crop failures of the early nineteenth century which had left the crofters destitute. It was said that the population was too high for the land to support but the landowners' desire to introduce profitable sheep farming was the main reason for the Clearances. Sheep farming was incompatible with crofting. Wool prices fell towards the end of the nineteenth century and many sheep farms were converted into sporting estates for affluent aristocrats or successful industrialists. This explains why so much of the present-day Highlands are bare, treeless semi-deserts and why the human settlements are confined to the coastal areas.

Lazy Beds
East Harris

'Lazy beds' are perhaps the most inappropriately named features in the landscape of agriculture as they represent a back-breaking attempt to wrest a living from a difficult environment. They were formed by cutting two parallel trenches approximately 2m (6ft) apart and piling the soil in a heap between them. Usually these raised beds were well fertilized with manure and seaweed and they provided a reasonable depth of well-drained soil above the water table. Very high yields could be obtained from these intensively worked plots which are found in profusion over the whole of the Outer Hebrides. The size of the population and the level of arable activity which once was carried out in the Outer Isles can only be judged by pondering the vast numbers of these abandoned lazy beds. As on the mainland, the people were cleared from this land to make way for sheep.

Crofts
Balallan, Lewis

The fields of Balallan overlook the hilly peninsula of Park, which in the 1820s and 1830s was cleared of its inhabitants by the landowner in order to establish a sheep farm, and subsequently converted into a sporting estate let to an English industrialist, despite the pleas of local crofters and landless cottars who requested leases there. A crofters' raid on Park was organized from Balallan in 1887 with the purpose of shooting as many deer as possible to feed the starving families, and also to reduce the profitability of the estate for recreational sport. It was hoped thus to 'persuade' the recalcitrant landowner to restore the land to the populace, some of whom were the grandchildren of the originally evicted tenants. This raid was one of the events which brought attention to the plight of the destitute landless in Lewis and led to 'the first of a continuing series of attempts to stimulate the Highland economy by means of judicious applications of financial assistance'.

Hector MacAulay
Crofter
Balallan, Lewis

Mr Hector MacAulay, on a blustery day in July between showers, was here completing haystacks made in the traditional manner on his croft.

Church of Our Lady of Braes Lochailort

Most Highland churches are simple buildings; their austerity adds to the power of their presence in the landscape. The history of the Christian faith in the area is, however, far from simple, and inextricably linked with temporal politics. A robustly independent, if contradictory, thread which runs through this history manifested itself in the joyful, although officially heretical, teachings of the early Celtic church, but also in the more recent support for the puritanical Free Church of Scotland.

Following the Reformation, the Protestant Church of Scotland succeeded the Roman Catholic as the established church. A further division took place in 1843 with the founding of the Free Church. At the time of the Clearances, the Church of Scotland became identified with the interests of the landowners. As a consequence, many crofters supported the breakaway Free Church. In Lewis, fewer than 500 people out of a population of 20,000 remained in the established church. The Free Church was to have, and still has, a significant effect on the character of Highland Society, especially in parts of the Hebrides.

Bowmore, Islay

The establishment of 'planned villages' in Scotland was a part of the general reorganization of estates which occurred in the period of agricultural 'improvement'. They were necessary as centres for rural industry and also to absorb the population displaced from the land as a result of enclosure and the establishment of large farm units. One hundred and thirty such villages were founded in the period 1770 to 1830 but very few of these were in the Highlands and Islands. Bowmore was one of these and it is significant that it was in Islay, one of the most fertile of the Hebridean isles. It is remarkable for its very wide principal street and for its imposing circular-plan parish church, of which it has been said that it was constructed thus, without corners, so that the 'Deil would have no place to lurk therein'.

Plockton

Plockton is a rare example of a West Highland planned village which was intended to stimulate a combination of crofting and small-scale fishing. It has a very well protected, almost landlocked, natural harbour but this dries out at low tide, which may have been the reason why the village failed to grow to its intended size. The very sheltered location, together with the warming effect of the Gulf Stream, have given Plockton a humid, balmy climate which has allowed its inhabitants to establish exotic trees and other plants there. On the rare days in summer when the sun shines from a cloudless blue sky, the atmosphere of the main street on the sandy beach becomes almost sub-tropical.

Duncraig Castle
Plockton

Duncraig Castle, on the opposite side of the small bay which forms the natural harbour at Plockton, was begun in 1841 and belonged to Sir Alexander Matheson, a merchant who amassed a fortune, it was said, in the opium trade between India and China. He was one of many wealthy businessmen who bought land in Scotland in the nineteenth century in the aftermath of the economic and social turmoil following the final defeat of the Jacobites and the breakdown of the clan system. It was said that he could walk from the Atlantic to the North Sea without setting foot off land which he owned. To his credit he resisted all Clearances from his estates, which is more than can be said of most of the clan chiefs who, despite having been served very well by their devoted clansmen, had no compunction in evicting them from their ancestral homelands, when it became economically advantageous to do so.

The Trossachs Hotel Loch Achray

The heartland of the 'romantic' Highlands was, and is, the Trossachs, and such was the popularity of the area following the publication of the early novels of Sir Walter Scott that a tourist industry sprang up there literally overnight. The Trossachs Hotel, 'a romantic confection to suit the wild landscape', is an essay in Scots Baronial Revival Architecture. It dates from 1852 and is well calculated, like the weather often experienced in the area, to appeal to the most Gothic of tastes.

Loch Achray Trossachs

From the perspective of the late twentieth century it can be seen that of all the enterprises which were begun in the aftermath of the 1745 Jacobite Rising, in the various attempts which were made to 'modernize' the Highlands, the only one which was to grow into a highly successful, high revenue-earning industry, was that of tourism and recreation. It is ironic that these were not activities which were initiated or even particularly encouraged by the worthy Commissioners who toiled so earnestly to bring a new prosperity to the area. They happened as a consequence of various factors: the romantic novels and poems of Walter Scott, which so appealed to the Victorian mind and which drew the Highlands of Scotland to the attention of the world; the attachment to the Highlands of Queen Victoria herself, who became a Highland landowner and made journeying to the area in the summer months a fashionable activity; the railway companies, which made such journeys possible; and, above all, the incomparable scenery of mountains and lochs such as is depicted here.

In the Highlands and Islands Now

Achiltibuie

The village of Achiltibuie and the surrounding country suffered much at the time of the Clearances and are now sparsely populated. Until recently the village had an active salmon fishing station and it still boasts a considerable smokery which produces smoked salmon and other products. Most of the fishing which is carried out from here now is for sport, however. Fishing parties, under experienced boatmen, set out for Loch Broom and the Minch in search of haddock, skate, shark, conger, tope and hus. Boatmen also take visitors to Tanera Mor, one of the Summer Isles, which is now uninhabited, but which once supported a population of seventy and a large fishing station. Today the Summer Isles are a place where seals and sea birds can breed in relatively undisturbed conditions and are consequently a paradise for naturalists.

A Commissioner of the Forfeited Estates, returning to the Highlands today after an absence of two hundred years, would find much at which to marvel. It is now possible to land on Barra in the Outer Hebrides a little over an hour after leaving Glasgow in a small plane, and to travel by road from Inverness to Edinburgh in around three hours. These improvements to communications are having a significant effect on the pattern of life. They have reduced the self-reliance and independence of the Highland communities and have made possible a 'lowland' lifestyle. They have also greatly increased the number of visitors who come to the area to enjoy its special, and now vulnerable, atmosphere; people from other areas have chosen to make their homes in the Highlands for the same reason. Many of the changes are recent and had our Commissioner returned to the area thirty years ago he might well have found that the most astonishing feature of the Highlands was the extent to which they had remained unchanged since the ending of the Jacobite wars.

The Highlander is still there and is still at loggerheads with the officials who would have him improve his lot. Many still practise the crofting way of life and are part farmer and part fisherman but, to an increasing extent, the revenue-earning activities are now more likely to be related to tourism: the former fisherman will be a holiday boatman who also tends a few lobster pots, and the farmer a guest-house proprietor. The fierce independence and disinclination to work harder than is necessary to provide the basic amenities of life can still be found, however, as can the love of story-telling, Gaelic poetry and song. In other words, the old Celtic spirit, which so infuriated the lowland Britons (both well- and not-so-well-intentioned) of the eighteenth century, is still very much alive – but for how long?

Plockton

The village of Plockton is one of the most picturesque in the Highlands. Although in the nineteenth century it did not grow to the size envisaged by the planners who founded it in 1801, it is in the present day one of the most successful communities in the Highlands. Many of the people who live in Plockton today are descended from the original inhabitants and their numbers have been swelled over the years by incomers who have been drawn by the incomparable scenery and the tranquillity of the area. Plockton may be an ideal place to retire to but it also has a growing child population, which is rare in the Highlands. It is not surprising therefore that it has an excellent primary school. What is perhaps out of the ordinary is that it is also the home of a college for further education. Education is in fact one of the main activities in Plockton today.

South Beach
Stornoway, Lewis

Stornoway is the principal town of the Western Isles. It possesses a sheltered anchorage on the east coast of Lewis and has been a trading and fishing port for many centuries. Seven hundred boats fished out of here during the summer season of 1898 but since then the industry has steadily declined and now only relatively few are engaged in this uncertain occupation, many of them in the inshore activities of crab and lobster fishing. The vast shoals of herring have gone, in part through overfishing, and such fish as are caught in local waters are now mostly landed at Lochinver, Ullapool or Mallaig, on the mainland, for easy road transport to the towns and cities of the south.

**Donald Macdonald
Retired Seaman
Ness, Lewis**

Mr Donald Macdonald, having
spent his working life as a
merchant seaman, has now retired
to his old home in Lewis. Because
of their maritime traditions, many
inhabitants of the Western Isles are
much more widely travelled than
the average summer visitor.

**Mr Mackinnon
Boatman
Loch Scavaig, Skye**

A small boat operates in summer
taking visitors from the pier at
Elgol to the head of Loch Scavaig,
at the feet of the Black Cuillins.
Here, the boatman draws his boat
alongside the rocks to allow his
passengers to alight. They now
have the choice of a brief excursion
to view the dramatic Loch
Coruisk, which lies within the
semi-circle of the mountains,
before returning by boat to Elgol,
or of walking the six miles or so
back along the beautiful and
rugged coast, by way of the
'Bad Step'.

Oban, Argyll

Oban is the gateway to the Hebrides. In the last two decades of the nineteenth century, following the coming of the railway, the town underwent an enormous expansion and became the main port in the south-western Highlands, used by fishermen, traders and increasing numbers of summer visitors to the area. All of these are still to be found in Oban today, which is as busy and bustling a town as ever. The name of MacBrayne has long been associated with commercial transport on the west coast of Scotland.

East Beach
Iona

'That man is little to be envied whose patriotism would not gain force upon the plain of Marathon, or whose piety would not grow stronger amid the ruins of Iona.' Thus spake Dr Samuel Johnson on seeing this enchanted isle, the cradle of Christianity in Scotland, in the late eighteenth century. It is possible that his reaction might be different were he to visit Iona today. The ruins of the old abbey and its associated monastic buildings have been rebuilt, and the massive influx of visitors, which occurs daily in the summer months, can have the effect of quenching the flickering flame of holiness in all but the staunchest of breasts. It is nevertheless possible still to find peace even in the most accessible parts of Iona, as is shown by the photograph, which was taken near the ferry pier and in the shadow of the abbey.

Loch of Stenness
Mainland, Orkney

The Orkney Isles are nearer to Norway than to Edinburgh. They were and are a meeting point of cultures. They lay on busy sea lanes in prehistoric times and have a greater density of ancient monuments than any other place in northern Europe. Throughout their history they have managed to retain a high degree of autonomy and today support a population which possesses great independence of spirit. The society is almost classless; there are few rich and few poor.

Despite its close association with the sea, Orkney, which possesses very fertile soil, is primarily a farming society. In late medieval times the land was gradually acquired by the rich and the powerful, and by the nineteenth century was owned mostly by wealthy landowners who lived outside the Islands. In the 1920s and 1930s, when returns from farming were low, the price of land fell and most tenant farmers were able to buy back their land. The Islands are now owned by those who live on and work them, which could account for the sense of vitality which is to be found there.

Stromness, Orkney

Stromness, originally called Hamnavoe, is a town whose existence is strongly linked to the sea. The houses present their gable-ends to it, in Scandinavian fashion, and most have their own piers jutting into the harbour. All kinds of vessels have called here. For nearly two hundred years Stromness had strong connections with the Hudson Bay Company, which at one time recruited 75 per cent of its workforce in Orkney, and its ships would spend two weeks every June in Stromness taking on supplies before setting out on the 'Northabout' route to 'Rupert's Land' (The North Atlantic route by way of Greenland for Quebec, Ontario, Manitoba and Saskatchewan).

Northton, Harris

The strip patterns of the nineteenth-century crofts are well shown here at Northton but, as elsewhere on the Islands, most crofts are now used solely for the pasturing of sheep or for growing a few rows of potatoes. A field of corn is now rarely seen and the milk which is delivered to most households comes from the mainland. All kinds of packaged foods are readily available, and the lively *ceilidh* (an informal evening of song and story) has been largely superseded by the torpor of watching television. In other words, the standard of living in the Islands is much higher now than hitherto, one of the benefits of improved communcations.

Iain McVean, Crofter
near Dalmally

Mr Iain McVean was here engaged in tending his immaculate garden, accompanied by Scott, his collie dog. Mr McVean started to work the family croft in 1928 with 'three cows, a borrowed horse and £12'. He later became known for his excellent pedigree herd of Welsh Black cattle, reluctantly parting with them only in 1985 at the age of 78. He has survived entirely without outside employment, which is unusual: most crofters are part-time, supplementing their income in other ways.

Although he and Mrs McVean have lived as crofters for many years, Iain McVean also has interesting tales to tell of other experiences, including of the days when he worked as a cabin boy on the steamer, the *Countess of Breadalbane*, which once plied the twenty-four miles between Lochawe station pier and the village of Ford at the other end of Loch Awe. The boat was replaced, as he remembers, in the late 1930s by a diesel-engined craft which was bolted together on the Clyde and rebuilt (rivetted) on the shore of Loch Awe, 'the noise of rivetting upsetting some of the natives'.

Shieldaig, Wester Ross

One of the most picturesque of the villages of Wester Ross, Shieldaig is situated near Beinn Alligin, the westernmost of the high mountains of Torridon, here shrouded in mist in the background. The wind-torn form of the native Scots pine in the foreground and the relative bareness of the landscape add poignancy to this relatively peaceful late winter scene.

Near Suilven, Assynt

The wild desolate landscape of Assynt is for many one of the most unspoiled and beautiful parts of Scotland. Others, however, point out that the bare and treeless expanses are not natural; one of the agencies preventing the growth of trees is that relative newcomer to the Highlands, the Cheviot sheep.

Annat, Wester Ross

This scene has a timeless quality; the sheep are following the crofter, who is carrying a bale of hay, all in the shadow of Liathach, 'the Grey One', one of the mightiest of the mountains of Torridon. The street lamps, the road, the caravan, the tractors and the mechanical scrap piled against the end of the barn locate this shot firmly in the late twentieth century, however.

Ian MacGregor, Piper Loch Lochy, Glen Mor

Ian MacGregor regularly plays the bagpipes for appreciative summer visitors in a layby on the road along the Great Glen. Before settling on this spot on Loch Lochy which, as he says 'has a special magic for myself and my grandmother, who comes up with me at least once a year', he often played in Glencoe, and he also travels with his pipes in North America. He comes from a piping family: he has his own bagpipe-making business, and was taught to play by his grandfather.

Creag Meagaidh Lochaber

Due to the richness of its plant and animal life, Creag Meagaidh was declared a Site of Special Scientific Interest in 1974, and is owned by Scottish National Heritage (formerly the Nature Conservancy Council). It is also a National Nature Reserve. Like most of the Highland Area, it has for centuries suffered from the effects of overgrazing by sheep and deer, the most obvious of these being the sparseness of the tree cover. In recent years the Nature Conservancy Council has had a policy of reducing the deer population to the level at which regeneration of the woodland is possible, so that animals and birds which are dependent on tree shelter will be encouraged to return to the area and a better balance of wildlife will occur. There is already evidence that this is proving to be successful and also that the quality of the deer stock is improving as a result of this management strategy. In this photograph a party of visitors is being taken up the mountain by the local warden.

The Black Wood of Rannoch

The 'Black' or 'dark' Wood of Rannoch is so named because it is composed mainly of Scots pine, being situated on the colder, north-facing, southern shores of Loch Rannoch where pine, rather than oak forest is the natural climax vegetation. Today it is managed by the Forestry Commission to allow regeneration of young pines and birch, as may be seen here. Much of Scotland would look like this if it were not for the unceasing nibbling of sheep and deer.

Crinan Harbour

Among the glories of the West Highlands of Scotland are the summer evenings in which the distant Hebridean Isles appear to float in a sea of gold. The characteristic smell of the seaweed, or 'tangle', the cry of the seabirds and the thin distant purring of an outboard motor complete the scene. In this picture we are looking westward across the Sound of Jura from Crinan, with the Isles of Jura and Scarba in the distance.

Crinan Canal

In the years following its construction the Crinan Canal achieved only a very limited commercial success and it might have been expected that in the harsh economic climate of the twentieth century it would have passed quietly into history or, at best, have been absorbed into the sterile world of the museum curator. By a happy combination of circumstances, however, it survived as a commercial enterprise into the era of mass prosperity, which brought the ownership of a cruising yacht within reach of a large section of society. As a result it has retained a vitality which would have been unimaginable had it become simply an 'ancient monument'. Depicted here is the busy scene at the Crinan Basin as yachts manoeuvre into the sea lock before setting off into the Hebridean seas.

Northern Corries
Cairngorms

The Cairngorms are the highest mountain mass in Britain and include six peaks of over 1200 m (4000 ft). Designated a National Nature Reserve, they offer a wide range of habitats for both flora and fauna and are particularly noted for their alpine plants.

Since the 1960s they have also been one of the prime skiing locations in Britain, and the cable-lifts (at the head of the car park in this picture), which operate throughout the year, provide access to the mountains for walkers and climbers as well as for skiers. In recent years much damage has been caused by the many boots which have trodden this highly sensitive and vulnerable upland area, and the overlapping but conflicting issues of leisure development and conservation have been hotly debated.

In this photograph the tarmac car park and access road to the ski-lifts become the burrow of a mechanical worm eating into the innards of the wilderness.

Sculpture Park
Glenshee

Glenshee is one of several popular skiing centres in the Highlands which, in recent years, have brought the leisure and conservation interests into conflict. At Glenshee a number of works of sculpture have appeared in the landscape in addition to the paraphernalia of ski-lifts and tows which are normally associated with this activity.

Inveraray

Inveraray has been the capital of Clan Campbell since they moved into Argyll in the fifteenth century. The present settlement is a planned village which was begun in 1743. The photograph shows Main Street, which has as its focus a splendid church designed by Robert Mylne. In the foreground is the silhouette of a fifteenth-century cross of the Iona School of carving. Inveraray was built at the very end of the Jacobite era at a time when Clan Campbell, which had carried the torch of mercantilism into the Gaelic Highlands, had finally triumphed over those who wished to preserve the traditional way of life. The architects which they employed drew their inspiration from the world of the English 'milordo' and the 'grand tour' and they created on the shores of Loch Fyne a settlement which conforms to the eighteenth-century English notion of a 'rule of taste'. It is much appreciated by present-day tourists.

Inveraray Castle

'An *opera-bouffe* country house of blue-slate stone', Inveraray Castle is the seat of the Dukes of Argyll. It was begun in 1744 to the designs of Roger Morris; the famous Adam family, father William and sons John and James, were also involved. It is a building which has always been strongly associated with the mercantilist culture of southern Britain, and remains so today.

Balemartine, Tiree

Tiree is the sunniest island in the Inner Hebrides. In this colourful scene it is possible to discern something of the difficulties of island life before the introduction of roll-on/roll-off ferries which can carry motorized fuel tankers. The red barrels contain petrol, blue denotes paraffin for lamps and heating, and yellow and black are the colours of diesel oil.

Scarista, Harris

Sheep are seen here grazing on the grass-covered remnants of lazy beds, on the *machair* of the west coast of Harris in the Outer Hebrides. This land was once intensively cultivated to support a large and thriving population, and could be so again.

SELECTED BIBLIOGRAPHY

Baird, W. J., *The Scenery of Scotland*, Edinburgh, National Museums of Scotland, 1988

Barrow, G. W. S., *Kingship and Unity: Scotland 1000– 1306*, Edinburgh, Edinburgh University Press, 1981

Carmichael, A. (Ed. A. Matheson), *Carmina Gadelica*, Edinburgh, Oliver & Boyd, 1958

Clapperton, C. M. (Ed.), *Scotland: A New Study*, Newton Abbot, David & Charles, 1983

Close-Brooks, Joanna, *Exploring Scotland's Heritage – The Highlands*, Edinburgh, HMSO, 1986

Cruden, Stewart, *The Scottish Castle*, Edinburgh, Spurbooks, 1981

Daiches, D. (Ed.), *A Companion to Scottish Culture*, London, Edward Arnold, 1981

Feachem, Richard, *Guide to Prehistoric Scotland*, London, Batsford, 1977

Fraser Darling, F. and Morton Boyd, J., *Natural History in the Highlands and Islands*, London, Bloomsbury Books, 1989

Geological Museum, *Britain Before Man*, London, HMSO, 1978

Grant, Alexander, *Independence and Nationhood: Scotland 1306– 1469*, London, Edward Arnold, 1984

Grant, I. F., *Highland Folk Ways*, London, Routledge & Kegan Paul, 1961

Holliday, F. (Ed.), *Wildlife of Scotland*, London, Macmillan, 1979

Hunter, J., *The Making of the Crofting Community*, Edinburgh, John Donald, 1976

Leneman, L. (Ed.), *Perspectives in Scottish Social History*, Aberdeen, Aberdeen University Press, 1988

Lenman, Bruce, *The Jacobite Risings in Britain 1689– 1746*, London, Methuen, 1980

Linklater, Eric, *The Prince in the Heather*, St Albans, Granada, 1976

MacDiarmid, Hugh, *The Islands of Scotland*, London, Batsford, 1939

Macdonald, Donald, *Lewis: A History of the Island*, Edinburgh, Gordon Wright, 1990

MacLean, Calum I., *The Highlands*, London, Batsford, 1959

MacLean, Charles, *The Fringe of Gold*, Edinburgh, Canongate, 1985

MacLean, Sorley, *O Choille gu Bearradh (From Wood to Ridge)*, Manchester, Carcanet Press, 1989

MacPhail, I. M. M., *The Crofters' War*, Stornoway, Acair, 1989

Murray, W. H., *The Islands of Western Scotland*, London, Eyre Methuen, 1973

Murray, W. H., *The Scottish Highlands*, Edinburgh, The Scottish Mountaineering Trust, 1976

Nethersole-Thompson, D. and Watson, A., *The Cairngorms*, Perth, Melvin Press, 1981

Ritchie, Anna, *Exploring Scotland's Heritage – Orkney and Shetland*, Edinburgh, HMSO, 1985

Ritchie, Graham and Anna, *Scotland: Archaeology and Early History*, London, Thames & Hudson, 1981

Ritchie, Graham and Harman, Mary, *Exploring Scotland's Heritage – Argyll and the Western Isles*, Edinburgh, HMSO, 1985

Ross, S., *Monarchs of Scotland*, Moffat, Lochar Publishing, 1990

Shepherd, Ian A. G., *Exploring Scotland's Heritage – Grampian*, Edinburgh, HMSO, 1986

Schei, Liv and Moberg, Gunnie, *The Orkney Story*, London, Batsford, 1985

Simpson, W. D., *Craigievar Castle*, Edinburgh, The National Trust for Scotland, 1978

Smout, T. C., *A History of the Scottish People 1560– 1830*, London, Collins, 1969

Smyth, A. P., *Warlords and Holy Men: Scotland AD 80– 1000*, Edinburgh, Edinburgh University Press, 1984

Streit, J., *Sun and Cross*, Edinburgh, Floris Books, 1984

Thompson, F., *The Western Isles*, London, Batsford, 1988

Thomson, D. S. (Ed.), *The Companion to Gaelic Scotland*, Oxford, Blackwell, 1983

Thomson, D. S., *An Introduction to Gaelic Poetry*, Edinburgh, Edinburgh University Press, 1990

Whittow, J. B., *Geology and Scenery in Scotland*, Harmondsworth, Penguin Books, 1977

Wormald, Jenny, *Court, Kirk, and Community: Scotland 1470– 1625*, London, Edward Arnold, 1981

Youngson, A. J., *After the Forty-Five*, Edinburgh, Edinburgh University Press, 1973

INDEX

Page numbers in *italics* refer to photographs